DALLAS MUSEUM OF ART

REVISED EDITION

gallery buffet
soup cookbook

DESIGN BY HUBLER-ROSEBURG ASSOCIATES, INC.
PHOTOGRAPHS BY BILL J. STREHORN AND DAVID WHARTON

ISBN NUMBER 0-9609622-1-2
Library of Congress Catalog Card No. 83-70905
Copyright© 1983 by Dallas Museum of Art
All Rights Reserved

First Edition, November 1977
Second Edition, January 1978
Third Edition, September 1978
Revised Fourth Edition, May 1983

Printed in the United States of America
Hart Graphics
Austin, Texas

BERTHE MORISOT
  Lady with a Muff

All work on this cookbook was done by a special committee of the Dallas Museum of Art League, an educational and volunteer organization of the museum.

In 1969 the Museum League opened, managed and staffed with volunteers a lunchroom called the Gallery Buffet at the museum. The Gallery Buffet is now professionally managed but the Museum League has continued to provide volunteers for its daily operation. The soups served there became famous in the area and the recipes often were requested. Because of these requests and because there are few cookbooks devoted exclusively to the preparation of soup, the idea for the **Gallery Buffet Soup Cookbook** was born.

This revised edition contains over twenty new soup recipes as well as new art work showing paintings of women and children from the museum's permanent collection.

All proceeds from the sale of this cookbook will be given to the Dallas Museum of Art to be used for the acquisition of works of art.

Mrs. Melvin L. Wellons
Mrs. James S. Cleaver

Editors

ACKNOWLEDGEMENTS

The Dallas Museum of Art League wishes to thank all those who contributed recipes to the first three printings of this cookbook and to this new edition. For devoting so much care, time and effort in testing those recipes, we are especially grateful to:

Mrs. Robert H. Bloom
Mrs. James S. Cleaver
Mrs. Burton C. Einspruch
Mrs. Richard A. Erb
Mrs. Perry E. Gross
Mrs. John P. Hall
Mrs. Roger Horchow
Mrs. Donald J. Malouf
Mrs. C. Thomas May
Mrs. Lawrence S. Pollock, Jr.
Mrs. Albert D. Roberts, Jr.
Mrs. Paul G. Wallof, Jr.
Mrs. Melvin L. Wellons
Mrs. James F. Williams
Mrs. Joseph D. Zimmerman

We also wish to thank Harry S. Parker III, Director of the Dallas Museum of Art, and Steven Nash, Assistant Director and Chief Curator, for their support and counsel.

Our special appreciation goes to artist Olivette Hubler, who once again graciously donated time and talent for the design of this new edition.

Introduction

Political propaganda or social record, formal presentation or intimate sketch, the portrait since ancient times has served many purposes and provided an important vehicle for artistic and cultural expression. From the striking realism found in representations of Egyptian Old Kingdom officials, to the icy classicism of Napoleonic imagery, to the nearly abstract stylizations of Cubist heads, portraiture runs a full gamut of moods and styles and tells us much about the individuals depicted, as well as the artists themselves. The Dallas Museum of Art is fortunate to number in its collection many examples of this special genre, and to accompany the present volume a selection has been made of 18th, 19th, and 20th century portraits of women and children. It is a group with much charm and visual attraction, although it also contains moments of great psychological penetration, and the level of artistic accomplishment is high throughout.

The earliest example in the group is Gilbert Stuart's *Portrait of Mrs. John Ashley* of 1798. One of a pair of portraits of the Ashleys by Stuart, it projects the sense of dignity and status that characterize his many depictions of prominent colonial families. Thomas Sully's *Portrait of Mrs. George H. Crossman,* a half-century later in date, perpetuates the Stuart tradition of quiet dignity but adds a full measure of 19th century realism. Mrs. Crossman impresses us not by her loftiness, but rather by the friendliness and approachability in her eyes and smile. Three other American portraits from around the end of the century, John Singer Sargent's *Portrait of Dorothy,* Thomas Eakins' *Miss Gertrude Murray,* and Mary Cassatt's *Sleeping Baby,* illustrate three new stylistic directions prominent by that time. Cassatt's pastel is an embodiment of the principles of color, light, and spontaneity so central to Impressionism, a movement in which she was the only American to participate in its early French phases. Sargent absorbed much from Impressionism but added a distinctive virtuosity of brushwork and paint handling, as is fully evident in the charming *Portrait of Dorothy,* a work that was praised when first exhibited for capturing the essence of youthful spirit. Eakins, on the other hand, was a master of realism and the psychological portrait, as we see so clearly in his somber study of his friend Gertrude Murray.

From across the Atlantic come Manet's *Portrait of Isabelle Lemonnier* and Berthe Morisot's *Lady with a Muff.* Painted only a year or two apart, they epitomize French Impressionist portraiture, with its air of fashionable elegance, its dashing spontaneity of brushwork, and its brilliant handling of tonal or chromatic variations.

The last three works lead us into the 20th century and demonstrate formal breakthroughs that helped inaugurate the modernist era. George Bellows, associated with the so-called Ashcan School, defied sentimental and academic conventions with fresh naturalism and his aggressive, simplified handling of structure, as seen in the famous portrait of his wife *Emma in a Purple Dress.* By contrast, Modigliani created a modern mode based on Cubist and primitive sources, which resulted in the elongated and faceted stylizations of his *Boy in Short Pants,* a rendering of an unidentified youth that is both ingratiating and severe. For Georges Rouault, painting was an intensely emotional, even religious experience. The dark, rich color and bold modeling of his *Woman's Head* reveal a type of expressionism that penetrates through surface appearance to inner, personal meanings.

All of these artists, through their individual portraits, contributed not only to the history of art but also to an understanding of human nature. We at the Dallas Museum of Art are glad to have the present book as a means of sharing with a wider audience their accomplishments.

Steven A. Nash
Assistant Director/Chief Curator

ILLUSTRATIONS

The illustrations in this book are a selection of paintings of women and children from the permanent collection of the Dallas Museum of Art.

Page

X

CONTENTS

xiv

HINTS FOR SOUPMAKING

Add a squeeze of fresh lime to chicken broth or vegetable soup.

Do not use the same amount of fresh herbs as dried. In most cases, 1 tablespoon of a fresh herb is equal to 1 teaspoon of a dried.

If soup is too salty, add half of a peeled, raw potato. If still too salty, add the other half. Remove before serving.

To remove fat from broth or stock:
1. Skim off fat with metal spoon, or
2. Lay paper towel on surface and, when saturated, remove and replace with a fresh towel, or
3. Use a lettuce leaf instead of a paper towel, or
4. Wrap a piece of ice in a paper towel and skim surface, or
5. Refrigerate broth overnight and remove congealed fat from surface on the following day.

Never allow liquid to boil when making stock. Fat and scum incorporate themselves into the stock causing it to become cloudy.

To clarify stock; Add 2 egg whites, lightly beaten, and the crushed shells of the eggs. Allow this to come to a boil and boil briskly for 2 minutes. Strain through 3 thicknesses of cheesecloth.

Never cover the soup kettle airtight unless its contents have cooled completely because the stock will sour.

Try using a coarse salt such as Kosher salt because it has a saltier taste. You might also try sea salt, which costs a bit more, but has a marvelous, briney taste.

A discriminating selection of seasonings such as curry, various bottled sauces (Tabasco, Worcestershire Sauce, B-V and steak sauces) will give new zest to canned soups.

Save all bones and poultry carcasses, scraps and giblets to add to stock pot. Also include leftover gravies and meat essences (see recipe for Pot-au-feu).

GARNISHES FOR SOUPS

Slices or tiny cubes of avocado.

Slivered almonds or chopped nuts.

Minced or sliced, hard-cooked egg.

Finely chopped watercress, parsley, chives, basil, dill or other fresh herbs.

Strips of pimiento, raw mushrooms, carrots, green onions or green pepper.

Paper thin slices of lemon, orange or lime.

Sliced chopped olives, green or ripe.

Grated or crumbled cheese.

Sour cream, whipped cream.

Croutons, dipped in melted butter, rolled in Parmesan cheese, and toasted.

Chopped radishes, minced onions.

A paste of olive oil and Parmesan cheese.

Croûtes (hard-toasted French bread):
Spread a cooky sheet with French bread rounds cut in ¾ inch thicknesses. Bake in a 325⁰ oven for about half an hour or until the rounds are thoroughly dried out and lightly brown. Halfway through the baking each side can be basted with a teaspoon of olive oil. After baking, each piece can be rubbed with cut garlic.
Note: These may be topped with grated Swiss or Parmesan cheese and run under the broiler.

Rouille (garlic, pimiento and chili pepper sauce):
The following sauce is passed separately with fish soups or bouillabaisse. Stir desired amount into each serving.

¼ C. canned pimientos
few drops Tabasco
1 medium-size, peeled potato that has been cooked in the soup
4 cloves garlic, pressed
1 t. basil, thyme or savory
4 to 6 T. olive oil
salt and pepper
2 or 3 T. hot soup

Place pimientos, Tabasco, potato, garlic, basil, thyme or savory in a bowl or mortar and pound ingredients for several minutes to form a sticky paste. Then pound or beat in the olive oil, drop by drop. Season to taste with salt and pepper. Just before serving, beat into the hot soup by driblets.

CHEDDAR CHEESE SOUP

¼ C. butter
½ C. onion, finely chopped
½ C. carrots, finely chopped
½ C. celery, finely chopped
¼ C. flour
1½ T. cornstarch
1 qt. chicken broth
1 qt. half and half cream
⅛ t. soda
2½ C. sharp cheddar cheese, grated and tightly packed
salt and white pepper
2 T. parsley, finely chopped

Melt butter in a large, heavy saucepan. Add the onions, carrots and celery and sauté until soft. Slowly stir in flour and cornstarch. Gradually add chicken broth and half and half cream, stirring constantly over low heat until smooth and thickened. Stir in soda and cheese and continue stirring until cheese is melted. Add salt and white pepper to taste. Garnish each serving with chopped parsley. Serves 8.

Cheddar Cheese Soup

Minestrone

Leek and Potato Soup

Mulligatawny Soup

Chicken Gumbo

Crab Bisque

Chilled Pimiento Soup

Cream of Spinach Soup with Crabmeat

Fresh Mushroom Soup

Garlic Soup

Split Pea Soup

gallery buffet soups

GILBERT STUART
  Portrait of Mrs. John Ashley

MINESTRONE (Italian)

¾ C. onion, chopped
¼ C. salt pork, diced
1 clove garlic, minced
¼ C. olive oil
1 T. dried basil
1 T. dried oregano
¼ C. parsley, minced
1½ C. canned tomatoes
1 C. hot water
¾ C. turnips and greens, diced
¾ C. carrots, diced
¾ C. zucchini, sliced
¾ C. raw potatoes, peeled and diced
¾ C. celery, diced
¾ C. cabbage, sliced
¼ C. navy beans, cooked
1 C. ham, chopped
½ C. uncooked macaroni
⅓ C. Parmesan cheese
salt and pepper to taste

Sauté the onion, salt pork and garlic in the olive oil. When wilted, add basil, oregano and parsley and stir. Add the tomatoes, hot water, turnips and greens, carrots, zucchini, potatoes, celery and cabbage and bring to a boil. Add more hot water to bring the soup to the consistency you prefer. It should be rather thick. Simmer about 30 minutes. Add the navy beans, ham, macaroni, cheese and seasonings at least 30 minutes before serving. Serves 8 to 10.

LEEK AND POTATO SOUP

8   leeks, white and light green parts only
1   stick butter
4   medium potatoes, peeled and finely diced
1   carrot, thinly sliced
4   C. chicken broth, heated
1   qt. water, heated
1   C. milk
salt and white pepper
chopped parsley

Cut leeks in half lengthwise and then crosswise in 1 inch pieces. Simmer gently in butter for about 10 minutes. Add potatoes, carrot, chicken broth and water. Season with salt and white pepper to taste. Cook over just enough heat to keep soup at low boil for 40 minutes or until potatoes can be mashed easily against sides of pan. Let cool slightly and put through blender. Return to stove. Stir in scant cup of milk. Adjust seasonings. Garnish each serving with chopped parsley. Serves 8.

MULLIGATAWNY SOUP

½ C. onion, finely chopped
3 T. butter
2½ T. flour
2 t. curry powder
1 qt. chicken broth, heated
1 pt. half and half cream
salt and white pepper
1 C. cooked chicken, cut up in thin slices
1 raw tart apple, peeled, cored and finely chopped
1 T. fresh parsley, chopped

In a large saucepan, sauté onion in butter until soft. Stir in flour and curry powder and cook about 2 minutes. Gradually stir in heated broth. Stir constantly until mixture thickens and is smooth. Stir in half and half cream. Season to taste with salt and white pepper. Add chicken slices and apple 10 minutes before serving. Adjust seasonings, if necessary. Garnish each serving with chopped parsley. Serves 6 to 8.

Note: Mulligatawny is a compatible first course with almost any lamb dish. It originally came from India and is at once both exotic and subtle, as well as beautiful. Have fun with your guests and see who can identify the surprise ingredient (apple)!

CHICKEN GUMBO

1   clove garlic, chopped
2   C. onion, chopped
2   C. celery, chopped
2   C. green pepper, seeded and chopped
½   C. fresh parsley, chopped
1   C. green onions (include tops), chopped
1   stick margarine
½   C. flour
6   C. chicken broth, heated
1   1 lb. bag frozen cut okra
2   C. canned tomatoes
1   C. rice, uncooked
4   C. cooked chicken, diced
salt and pepper to taste
V-8 juice and additional chicken broth for thinning mixture
      if it becomes too thick

Sauté garlic, onion, celery, green pepper, parsley and green onions in margarine. Slowly add flour and cook for 3 minutes. Gradually stir in heated broth. Add okra, tomatoes, rice and chicken. Add salt and pepper to taste. Cook 20 to 30 minutes longer. Adjust seasonings. If soup becomes too thick, thin with mixture of half V-8 juice and half chicken broth. Serves 10.

CRAB BISQUE

2   T. onion, minced
¼   C. margarine
¼   C. flour
½   t. dry mustard
1   qt. milk, heated
2   C. half and half cream, heated
1   C. fresh crabmeat (carefully picked over to remove
    bits of shell and cartilage)
salt and white pepper
fresh parsley, chopped

Sauté onion in margarine until onion is soft. Add flour and mustard and cook, stirring, for 2 minutes. Slowly stir in heated milk and half and half cream and allow to thicken. Add crabmeat. Season to taste with salt and white pepper. Garnish with chopped parsley. Serves 4 to 6.

CHILLED PIMIENTO SOUP

1   4 oz. jar pimientos
2   T. minced onion
1   can Campbell's Cream of Chicken Soup, undiluted
2   C. light cream
salt and white pepper to taste
chopped chives

Combine first 3 ingredients in blender and blend until smooth. Add cream and salt and white pepper to taste. Refrigerate for at least 3 hours or until very cold. Garnish each serving with chopped chives. Serves 4.

CREAM OF SPINACH SOUP WITH CRABMEAT

2   packages frozen, chopped spinach
4   slices white onion
6   C. chicken broth
6   T. butter
2   T. flour
salt and white pepper to taste
2   C. half and half cream
1   C. fresh crabmeat (carefully picked over to remove bits of shell and cartilage)
½ t. nutmeg

Cook spinach (and onions) according to directions on spinach package. Drain thoroughly. Combine with just 2 cups of the chicken broth and put through blender until puréed. Melt butter in a large saucepan. Stir in flour and salt and white pepper until blended. Gradually stir in the remaining 4 cups of chicken broth and bring to boil, stirring constantly. Add puréed spinach mixture and cook over low heat for 10 minutes. Stir in half and half cream and crabmeat and heat but do not boil. Add nutmeg. Taste for seasoning. Serves 8 to 10.

FRESH MUSHROOM SOUP

15 green onions (including tender green tops),
   chopped fine
¾ C. butter
½ C. flour
salt and white pepper
7 C. chicken broth, heated
1½ lbs. fresh mushrooms, washed, trimmed and sliced
2 C. half and half cream

Sauté onion in butter for about 3 minutes. Add flour and salt and white pepper to taste. Heat for about 10 minutes, stirring constantly. Slowly add heated chicken broth and bring to boil. Stir in mushrooms (reserving some for garnish) and cook 10 minutes more. Put through blender until smooth. Return to stove and stir in half and half cream. Heat but do not let boil. Garnish each serving with reserved mushroom slices. Serves 8.

GARLIC SOUP

20 pods of garlic, peeled and sliced
4   T. butter
2   fresh tomatoes, peeled, seeded and diced
½ C. carrots, scraped and sliced
¼ C. celery, sliced
¼ C. onion, diced
4   C. chicken broth
1   egg, separated
½ T. cider vinegar
salt and pepper to taste

In a large saucepan, sauté the garlic in butter until very soft. Stir in the tomatoes and cook briefly. Add carrots, celery and onion and cook until onion is soft. Stir in broth and simmer, uncovered, until vegetables are cooked through. Remove from heat. In a separate bowl, combine egg yolk and vinegar and beat slightly. Carefully stir in 2 or 3 ladlesful of the soup mixture. Stir slowly back into soup a little at a time. Without beating beforehand, whisk egg white into soup mixture. Season to taste with salt and pepper. Reheat, if necessary, but do not allow to boil. Serves 4.

Note: Don't be put off by the title. This is an aromatic, beautiful and delicious soup. When the garlic is boiled, it loses the familiar pungency and instead flavors the soup subtly and almost indefinably.

SPLIT PEA SOUP

1   lb. dried green peas
1   onion, chopped fine
4   medium-size carrots, chopped fine
¼   stalk celery, chopped fine
1   small garlic clove, chopped fine
2   C. lean cured ham, cubed (a meaty ham bone may
    be substituted)
pinch of thyme
salt and pepper to taste
2   qts. water

Wash peas and remove imperfect ones. Soak overnight, well covered, in water. Drain and wash peas again in fresh water. Combine first 8 ingredients in a heavy kettle and cover with the 2 qts. of water. Cook about 2 hours or until peas are tender. Add more water if soup becomes too thick. If using ham bone, remove and cut meat from bone into small pieces. Return meat to kettle. Correct seasonings. Serves 8 to 10.

Black Bean Soup

Lentil Soup

Pot-au-feu

Scotch Broth

Sunday Night Fireside Soup

Savory Cabbage Soup

Brunswick Stew

Old Country Borscht

Cold Day Potage

hearty soups

BLACK BEAN SOUP

1   C. dried black beans
½   t. soda
4   pts. water
2   T. meat extract (B-V)
2   stalks celery, chopped
1   bay leaf, crumbled
½   lb. lean cured ham, cubed
1   T. parsley, chopped
1   t. coarsely ground black pepper
1   t. fine herbs
1   t. paprika
2   medium onions, chopped
1   green pepper, seeded and chopped
1   clove garlic, crushed
⅓   lb. salt pork
1   C. Chianti (or any dry red wine)
salt to taste
6   to 8 lemon slices
2   hard-boiled eggs, grated

Wash beans and remove imperfect ones. Soak overnight, well covered, in water to which the soda has been added. Wash beans again in fresh water to remove soda. Drain and put in soup kettle with 4 pints water and the meat extract. Put celery, bay leaf and ham also in kettle. Add parsley, pepper, garlic and salt pork in skillet over slow fire. Pour grease and all into the soup. Place lid on kettle and simmer for at least four hours. Cool to lukewarm. Put soup through blender in batches. Return to stove and add wine. Add salt to taste. Stir slowly over slow fire but DO NOT BOIL. Garnish each serving with a lemon slice and some of the grated egg. Serves 6 to 8.

This marvelous, hearty winter soup is even better on the second or third day.

LENTIL SOUP

1	lb. dried lentils
¼	lb. bacon, diced
2	medium onions, thinly sliced
2	carrots, scraped and thinly sliced
1	C. celery, thinly sliced
2	bay leaves
¼	t. dried thyme

salt and pepper to taste

2	qts. water
1	large potato, peeled and grated
1	meaty ham bone

Soak lentils overnight in plenty of water to cover. Drain. In a large kettle sauté bacon, onions and carrots until onions are golden. Add the drained lentils, celery, bay leaves, thyme, salt, pepper and the 2 quarts of water. Add the grated potato and the ham bone. Cover and simmer for 3 or 4 hours. Discard bay leaves. Cut meat from ham bone and return to kettle. Adjust seasonings. Reheat, if necessary. Serves 6 to 8.

POT-AU-FEU

1½ to 2 lbs. beef hind shank for stew
leftover knuckle bones or other bones from roast (or remains of roast chicken or turkey)
2 or 3 medium-size onions, each studded with a clove
1 celery stalk with leaves, chopped
4 to 6 whole peppercorns
1 qt. water (or enough to cover)
2 T. salt
¼ t. thyme
¼ t. basil
1 bay leaf
1 T. fresh parsley, minced

any leftover brown sauce or gravy (any amount)
2 C. dry table wine
1 to 2 C. leftover beans, rice or pasta (or ½ C. uncooked rice or elbow macaroni)
1 lb. uncooked boneless stewing meat (veal or pork)
any leftover cooked meat, diced
1 C. diced yellow vegetables (carrots, rutabaga or parsnips)
2 or 3 leeks (white parts only), chopped
2 C. green vegetables (green beans or peas)

Place beef hind shank in kettle with leftover bones from roast meat or poultry. Add onions, celery, peppercorns, water, salt, thyme, basil, bay leaf and parsley. Cover pot and bring to a boil. Simmer for 3 hours, skimming surface when necessary. Remove the meat, reserving broth in kettle, and trim off the edible portions and save. Strain the broth and return to the kettle with the trimmed meat. Add the leftover sauce or gravy. Add the wine, beans or rice or pasta. Add the stewing meat and the leftover cooked meat. Cook for about 45 minutes. Add the yellow vegetables, leeks and green vegetables. Cook for about 20 minutes or until the vegetables are tender. Adjust seasonings. Serves 8 to 10.

Note: This is a traditional French soup made from leftover sauces, gravies and cooked meat.

SCOTCH BROTH

5   lbs. lamb bones
2   lbs. fatless, boneless shoulder of lamb, diced very small
2   lbs. beef bones
1   chicken (approximately 5 lbs.)
8   qts. cold water (use more if necessary)
1   C. large pearl barley
2   C. diced small yellow turnips
1   C. diced carrots
1   C. diced leeks, white part only
1   C. diced celery
½ C. diced onion
salt and pepper to taste
dash of thyme
chopped parsley

Make stock by placing lamb bones, diced lamb, beef bones, chicken and water in large kettle and cooking until meat is tender. Strain stock which should have cooked down to about 6 quarts. Add all the remaining ingredients except the seasonings and the parsley to the stock. Simmer for 2½ hours. Season to taste with salt, pepper and thyme. Garnish with chopped parsley. Serves 12 or more.

SUNDAY NIGHT FIRESIDE SOUP

1 lb. sausage meat
4 C. water
2 15¼ oz. cans red kidney beans, drained
1 lb. 13 oz. can tomatoes
1 onion, chopped
1 large bay leaf
½ clove garlic, minced
2 t. salt
⅛ t. black pepper
½ t. thyme
⅛ t. caraway seed
a pinch of crushed red pepper
1 C. raw potatoes, peeled and diced
1 small green pepper, with seeds removed, chopped

Brown sausage meat in a skillet. Drain the sausage and crumble it. In a kettle combine the sausage meat with the water, red kidney beans, tomatoes, onion, bay leaf, garlic, salt and black pepper, thyme, caraway seed and red pepper. Simmer the mixture for 1 hour. Add the potatoes and green pepper. Simmer, covered, for another 20 minutes. Adjust seasonings and serve. Serves 8.

THOMAS SULLY
Portrait of Mrs. George H. Crossman

SAVORY CABBAGE SOUP

2   lbs. beef bones
1   C. onion, chopped
3   carrots, peeled and coarsely chopped
2   cloves garlic, chopped
1   bay leaf
2   lbs. beef short ribs
½   beef brisket (about 2 to 3 lbs. of meat)
1   t. thyme
½   t. paprika
8   C. water
8   C. white cabbage, coarsely shredded
2   1 lb. cans tomatoes
2   t. salt (or less)
½ to ¾ t. Tabasco
3   T. sugar (optional)
¼   C. fresh parsley, chopped
3   T. lemon juice
1   package (1 lb.) sauerkraut, rinsed and drained
sour cream

Place beef bones, onion, carrots, garlic and bay leaf in roasting pan. Top with short ribs and brisket. Sprinkle with thyme and paprika. Roast, uncovered, in 450° oven until browned. Transfer meat and vegetables to a large kettle. To this add water, cabbage, tomatoes, salt, Tabasco and sugar. Bring to a boil. Cover and simmer until meat is tender. Skim off fat. Add parsley, lemon juice and sauerkraut. Cook, uncovered for 1 hour. Remove meat from bones and cut into bite size pieces. Return meat pieces to soup and cook 5 minutes longer. Serve with sour cream. Serves 8 to 10.

Note: To strengthen stock, bouillon cubes, leftover gravies or any essence of meat can be added.

BRUNSWICK STEW

1   6 lb. stewing hen or 2 broiler-fryers (3 lbs. each)
2   large onions, sliced
2   C. fresh or frozen okra, sliced
4   C. fresh tomatoes, peeled and chopped (or 2 1 lb. cans tomatoes)
2   C. fresh or frozen lima beans
3   medium potatoes, peeled and diced
4   C. fresh or frozen corn cut from cob
3   t. salt
1   t. pepper
1   t. sugar
1   T. Worcestershire Sauce
1   T. paprika
1   T. lemon juice
Tabasco
fresh parsley, chopped

Simmer chicken in 3 quarts water (for a thin stew) or 2 quarts water (for a thick stew) until tender. Remove chicken from broth. Skin, bone and cut into pieces. Add onions, okra, tomatoes, lima beans, potatoes and corn to broth. Simmer until lima beans and potatoes are tender. Stir occasionally to prevent scorching. Add chicken pieces, salt, pepper, sugar, Worcestershire Sauce, paprika, lemon juice and Tabasco to taste. Taste and adjust seasonings. Garnish with chopped parsley. Serves 8 to 10.

Note: It is a rule in some tidewater homes never to eat Brunswick Stew on the day it is made. The flavor improves if it is left to stand overnight and reheated the next day.

OLD COUNTRY BORSCHT

6   C. water or beef broth (more may be needed
    before serving)
1   lb. beef brisket, sliced in narrow strips
2   onions, sliced
2   stalks celery, sliced in narrow strips
2   C. fresh beets, pared and sliced
1½ C. carrots, pared and sliced
1   small head of cabbage, cut into narrow wedges
1   bay leaf
1   T. salt

1   C. fresh beets, pared and grated
¾   C. tomato paste (or a 6 oz. can)
2   T. cider vinegar
1   T. sugar
salt to taste
1   C. sour cream

On the day before:
In a large kettle, place first 9 ingredients. Simmer,
covered, for 2 hours. Add grated beets, tomato paste,
vinegar, sugar and salt. Simmer, covered, for 15 or 20
minutes. Remove from stove and let cool. Refrigerate
until following day.

To serve:
Skim any fat from surface of soup. Bring soup to a boil
over medium heat. Lower heat and simmer, covered,
for 10 minutes. Mixture may need thinning with broth
or water. Garnish each serving with a dollop of sour
cream. Serves 4 to 6.

COLD DAY POTAGE

2 lbs. dried Great Northern (white) beans
water (enough to cover beans)
2 large smoked sausage rings, chopped
2 large onions, chopped
3 carrots, chopped
1 bunch parsley, chopped
1 T. sugar
2 T. Lawry's Seasoned Salt (more if needed)
cracked black pepper to taste

Garnish:
  Monterrey Jack cheese, grated
  green onions, chopped
  Jalapeño peppers, chopped

Wash beans and remove imperfect ones. Soak overnight, well covered in water. Drain and wash beans again in fresh water. Combine ingredients, cover with water and cook until beans and vegetables are tender. If necessary, add more water while beans are cooking. Correct seasonings. To serve, garnish with the grated cheese, chopped green onions and chopped jalapeños. Serves 10.

Chicken Broth

Beef Stock

Veal Stock

Fish Stock

Enriched Canned Chicken Broth

Enriched Canned Beef Bouillon

Tomato Bouillon

Red Caviar Madrilène

broths, stocks, & clear soups

CHICKEN BROTH

1   2½ lb. chicken or 3 lbs. of chicken pieces
1   onion, quartered
2   stalks celery with leaves
2   carrots
5   sprigs fresh parsley
4   chicken bouillon cubes
½   C. dry white wine or dry white vermouth
salt and pepper to taste

Place all ingredients in a large kettle and cover with cold water. Bring to a boil. Simmer, covered, until chicken is tender (about 1 hour). Remove chicken from kettle. Remove meat from bones and set aside for another use. Return skin and bones to kettle and simmer for another 2 hours adding more water, if necessary. Strain the broth and skim fat from top. This broth can be frozen for future use. Makes 2 or more quarts.

BEEF STOCK

3　qts. of beef meat and bones (see note)
2　t. salt
cold water
2　carrots
2　onions, quartered
2　celery stalks

The following tied in cheesecloth:
¼　t. thyme
1　bay leaf
8　sprigs fresh parsley
2　cloves garlic
2　whole cloves

Place meat and bones in a large kettle. Cover with water making sure water comes several inches above. Set over moderate heat. As the liquid comes slowly to the simmer, scum will start to rise. Remove it with a wooden spoon or ladle. After scum is removed, add remaining ingredients and more water if liquid does not cover the ingredients by a full inch. When the liquid is simmering again, skim as necessary. Partially cover kettle, leaving space for steam to escape. Liquid should barely simmer for 4 to 5 hours or more. Add more water if liquid evaporates below level of the ingredients. Never allow liquid to boil as stock will become cloudy. Cooking may be stopped at anytime and continued later. Stock should be strained. Yields 2 to 3 quarts.

Note: Stock may be made from bones alone, but it will have more character if some meat is included. Ideal proportions are about half and half.

VEAL STOCK

3   lbs. lean, raw veal shank meat
4   lbs. cracked, raw veal bones
cold water
2   t. salt
2   carrots
2   onions, quartered
2   stalks celery

The following tied in cheesecloth:
¼   t. thyme
1   bay leaf
8   sprigs fresh parsley
2   garlic cloves

Place the meat and bones in a large kettle. Cover with cold water. Bring to a boil and boil slowly for 5 minutes. Drain. Rinse the bones and meat under cold water to remove the scum. Also rinse the kettle. Place the bones and meat back in the kettle. Cover again with cold water. Bring to the simmer and skim as necessary. Add rest of ingredients and simmer for 4 or 5 hours or more. Strain stock. Makes 2 to 3 quarts.

FISH STOCK

6   lbs. very fresh, very clean fish bones (preferably with heads left on)
4   qts. water
2   C. dry white wine
2   onions, peeled and cut into eighths (about 1½ C.)
1½ C. coarsely chopped celery tops
2   cloves garlic, quartered
1   bay leaf
12 peppercorns
salt to taste
4   sprigs fresh parsley
2   sprigs fresh thyme or 1 t. dried thyme

Combine all the ingredients and bring to a boil. Simmer for 20 minutes (cook longer if a stronger stock is desired). Strain. Discard the solids. Makes about 4½ quarts.

Note: Leftover stock may be frozen.

ENRICHED CANNED CHICKEN BROTH

2   C. canned chicken broth, undiluted
3   T. onions, chopped
3   T. carrots, chopped
3   T. celery, chopped
½   C. dry white wine or ⅓ C. dry white vermouth
3   sprigs fresh parsley
⅓   bay leaf
pinch of thyme
salt and pepper to taste

Simmer the chicken broth with the vegetables, wine and herbs for 30 minutes. Strain. Season to taste.

ENRICHED CANNED BEEF BOUILLON

2   C. canned beef bouillon, undiluted
3   T. onions, minced
3   T. carrots, minced
3   T. celery, minced
½   C. dry red wine, dry white wine or dry white vermouth
several sprigs of fresh parsley
⅓   bay leaf
⅛   t. thyme
salt and pepper to taste

Simmer the beef bouillon with the vegetables, wine and herbs for 30 minutes. Strain. Season to taste.

TOMATO BOUILLON

4 C. tomato juice
2 cans beef consommé, undiluted
4 whole cloves
8 peppercorns
half of a bay leaf
½ t. salt
pinch of sweet basil
1 small onion, chopped fine
1 or 2 celery tops
parsley sprig
thin slices of raw cauliflower

In a saucepan combine tomato juice and consommé. Add remaining ingredients except cauliflower and simmer for 30 minutes. Strain through 2 layers of cheesecloth. Adjust seasonings. Reheat, if necessary. Garnish each serving with a cauliflower slice. Serves 4 to 6.

RED CAVIAR MADRÌLENE

2 T. (2 envelopes) unflavored gelatin
½ C. cold water
2 C. tomato juice, strained
½ t. onion, grated
2 C. clear beef, veal or chicken stock
slice of lemon rind
salt and pepper
lemon juice
sherry
Worcestershire Sauce
2 oz. red caviar
6 T. sour cream
¼ C. chives, chopped

Dissolve gelatin in cold water according to package directions. In a saucepan combine tomato juice, onions, stock and lemon rind. Bring to a boil. Add the softened gelatin to the hot stock mixture and stir until it is thoroughly dissolved. Strain the mixture. Season to taste with salt, pepper, lemon juice, sherry and Worcestershire Sauce. Chill the mixture in 6 individual bouillon cups until almost set. Stir a teaspoon of caviar into each cup. Do this very carefully so as not to break eggs. Chill until soup is set. Just before serving, put a tablespoon of sour cream on each serving and sprinkle with the chopped chives. Serves 6.

Mushroom Soup

Asparagus Soup

Summer Squash Soup

Velvet Acorn Squash Bisque

Broccoli Soup

Leek and Pear Soup

Corn Chowder

Chilled Fresh Tomato Soup

Country French Bean Soup

Country French Bean Soup with
Lemon and Herbs

Javier's Black Bean Soup

Tiffany's Bean Pot Soup

Garden Fresh Vegetable Soup

vegetable soups

MUSHROOM SOUP

¾ lb. fresh mushrooms
6   C. chicken broth, preferably homemade
2   egg yolks
½ C. sour cream
1   t. dry sherry
salt and pepper to taste
2   T. fresh parsley, chopped

Wash mushrooms thoroughly. Simmer in chicken broth until tender (about 30 minutes). Put mixture through blender at slow speed. This will have to be done in batches because of the quantity. Beat egg yolks with the sour cream. Return mushroom mixture to stove and add egg yolks and sour cream, mixing thoroughly. Add sherry and season to taste with salt and pepper. Garnish each serving with parsley. Serves 6 to 8.

EDOUARD MANET
  Portrait of Isabelle Lemonnier

ASPARAGUS SOUP

¾ C. onions, sliced
4 T. butter
2½ to 3 lbs. fresh asparagus
6 C. water
4 T. flour
1 C. milk
salt and white pepper to taste
3 egg yolks
⅔ C. heavy cream

In a large saucepan, sauté the onions in butter until soft.
Cut off the tips of each asparagus stalk and set aside.
Cut off about ¼ inch of the butt end of each stalk. Peel
the stalk and slice into 1 inch pieces. Cook in 6 cups
boiling salted water for about 5 minutes. Remove stalks
from water with slotted spoon, reserving liquid. Add
stalks to onion mixture. Cover and cook for 5 minutes.
Meanwhile, bring reserved liquid back to boil, add
asparagus tips and cook until tender (about 8 to 10
minutes). Again reserving liquid, remove tips with slotted spoon and set aside. Stir flour into vegetable mixture. Remove from heat and slowly add asparagus liquid, stirring constantly. Return to heat, cover and simmer for 25 to 30 minutes or until asparagus is very
tender. Stir in milk and salt and white pepper. Purée
the mixture in a blender or food mill, strain and return
to saucepan. In a separate bowl, mix the egg yolks and
cream. Carefully blend in 2 or 3 ladlesful of soup mixture. Stir back into saucepan. Carefully add the
asparagus tips so as not to break them. Reheat, if
necessary but do not allow to boil. Correct seasonings.
Serves 6 to 8.

SUMMER SQUASH SOUP

1 ½ lbs. summer (yellow) squash
2   C. chicken broth (preferably homemade)
6   T. butter
Lawry's Seasoned Salt
6   green onions (use both white and green parts)
2   heaping T. flour
2   C. half and half cream, warmed
1   C. milk (or more)
½   t. sugar
pepper to taste
2   T. chopped parsley

Scrub squash and slice. Put squash in pan with chicken broth. Add 2 T. butter and season with a few dashes of the seasoned salt and cook until squash is tender. As squash is cooking, chop up the green onions and sauté them in ½ stick of butter until tender. Add flour to make a roux. Cook about 2 minutes and then add warmed half and half cream. Use a wire whisk to make white sauce. Let the sauce thicken over low heat, stirring often. Add squash mixture to pot. When thickened again, put mixture through blender. Return to stove and add milk until desired thickness is reached. Add sugar and pepper. Correct seasonings. Garnish with chopped parsley. Serves 6.

VELVET ACORN SQUASH BISQUE

3 T. butter
1 C. onion, finely chopped
1 C. carrot, grated
salt and white pepper to taste
2 medium potatoes, peeled and cubed
2 acorn squash, peeled and cubed
4 C. strong chicken broth
½ C. heavy cream
½ C. milk
cayenne pepper

Melt the butter in a saucepan. Add the onion, carrot, salt and white pepper. Cook over low fire until soft, stirring often. Add the potatoes and squash. Pour in the chicken broth and simmer, covered, over low heat for about 25 minutes or until all the vegetables are tender. Purée in blender. Return to stove. Stir in the cream and milk. Taste for seasoning and reheat. Sprinkle each serving with a dash of cayenne pepper. Serves 4 to 6.

BROCCOLI SOUP

3   to 4 C. fresh broccoli, chopped (chopped frozen
    broccoli may be substituted)
2   C. water
6   T. butter
½   C. onion, chopped
1   T. chicken instant bouillon
2   C. heavy cream
salt and pepper to taste
½   C. Gruyère cheese, finely grated, for garnish

If using fresh broccoli stems, be sure to peel them first.
In a food processor fitted with the steel blade, purée
the broccoli adding enough of the water to make a nice
purée. In a large saucepan, melt butter and sauté onion
until it is golden. Add broccoli purée and sauté, stirring
constantly, until broccoli is cooked. Stir in remaining
water. Mix in chicken instant bouillon and simmer for
about 15 minutes. Add cream and salt and pepper to
taste. Reheat. Garnish each serving with grated cheese.
Serves 4 to 6.

LEEK AND PEAR SOUP

3   C. leeks (white and light green parts only), cleaned and sliced
6   T. butter
3   fresh pears, peeled, cored and chopped (use 4 pears if you wish a fruitier taste)
6   C. chicken broth, strained through fine sieve
3   t. fresh summer savory, chopped (or 1 t. dried)
salt and white pepper to taste

In a large heavy saucepan, sauté leeks in butter for about 10 minutes, stirring often. Add pears and cook, stirring, for another 5 minutes. Add chicken broth and summer savory and bring to boil. Reduce heat and simmer, uncovered, for 20 minutes. In batches, purée the mixture in the blender. Transfer mixture back to cleaned saucepan. Season to taste with salt and white pepper. Reheat, if necessary. Garnish each serving with a sprinkle of summer savory. Serves 6 to 8.

Note: This is a delicate and light Nouvelle Cuisine soup with the subtle flavor of fresh pears.

CORN CHOWDER

3   oz. salt pork, cubed
1   large onion, chopped
1   rib of celery, chopped
1½ C. raw potatoes, diced
2   C. chicken broth
1   C. water
2   C. cream style corn
2   C. milk
¼   C. butter
salt and white pepper to taste

Fry pork until brown. Add onion and cook over medium heat for 5 minutes, stirring often. Add celery, potatoes, chicken broth and 1 cup water and cook until potatoes are done. Add corn and heat 5 minutes, stirring occasionally. Heat milk and butter together and add to the soup. Season with salt and pepper to taste and serve hot.
Serves 6.

CHILLED FRESH TOMATO SOUP

6 C. peeled and finely chopped fresh tomatoes
1 medium onion, grated
¾ C. lemon juice
1 t. vinegar
1 t. celery seed
salt to taste
6 T. mayonnaise
curry powder
chopped parsley

Combine tomatoes, onion, lemon juice, vinegar and celery seed. Mix well. Season with salt. Pour into freezer tray and freeze to a mush (about 1 hour). Serve half frozen. Top each serving with a dollop of mayonnaise that has been seasoned with curry and chopped parsley. Serves 6.

COUNTRY FRENCH BEAN SOUP

2   celery stalks, sliced
1   medium-size onion, sliced
1   medium-size leek, sliced (use only the white and
    light green parts)
3   T. butter
8   C. liquid (4 C. chicken broth, 4 C. beef broth)
1½ C. washed flageolets or white beans of any type
1   bay leaf
1   large clove garlic, unpeeled
salt and white pepper to taste
chopped parsley

In a heavy saucepan, sauté the celery, onion and leek
in the butter for 5 minutes or until the vegetables are
limp but not browned. Add the liquid and bring to a boil.
Add the beans, bay leaf, garlic and salt and white pepper. Bring rapidly to a boil again, uncovered, and boil
exactly 2 minutes. Remove from heat, cover saucepan
and set aside for 1 hour. Bring to a boil again. Lower
heat and simmer slowly, partially covered, for 1½ to
2 hours or until beans are thoroughly tender. Add more
liquid if needed. Discard bay leaf. Squeeze contents of
garlic clove into mixture. Adjust seasonings. Garnish
each serving with chopped parsley. Serves 4 to 6.

COUNTRY FRENCH BEAN SOUP WITH LEMON AND HERBS

Use ingredients from preceding recipe for **Country French Bean Soup**, plus:

salt, white pepper and nutmeg to taste
2   egg yolks
½ C. heavy cream (more cream or milk may be
     needed during the cooking process)
juice of 1 lemon
4   T. fresh basil, tarragon or parsley, minced (or 1
     T. dried)
Optional: homemade croutons

Follow preceding recipe for **Country French Bean Soup.** After discarding bay leaf and squeezing garlic into soup, put mixture through a food mill or food processor fitted with the steel blade. Return mixture to cleaned pan and bring to simmer. In a separate bowl, blend the yolks and the cream with a wire whip. By dribbles, blend in several ladlesful of the hot soup. Pour this mixture back into the soup and bring to just below a simmer. If the soup is too thick, thin with cream or milk. Remove from heat and stir in lemon juice and herbs. Season with salt, white pepper and nutmeg to taste. If necessary, reheat but do not allow to boil. Garnish each serving with minced herbs (and homemade croutons, if desired). Serves 4 to 6.

JAVIER'S BLACK BEAN SOUP

2   C. black beans
6   C. water (more may be needed during the cooking process)
½   onion, chopped
2   garlic cloves, chopped
2   T. olive oil
1   T. chicken instant bouillon
salt and black pepper to taste
1   ripe avocado, peeled, seeded and sliced
½   C. Monterrey Jack cheese, grated
1   T. fresh cilantro (if available), chopped. Do not use dried.

In a large heavy saucepan, drop beans into boiling water. Bring rapidly back to boil and continue boiling for 2 minutes. Remove from heat and let the beans soak, covered, in the water for 1 hour. (The beans will continue to cook in the heated water.) Meanwhile, sauté the onion and garlic in the olive oil until the onion is golden brown. Add to the bean mixture. Time your procedure so that the onion and garlic are added immediately after the bean-soaking process is completed. Simmer over medium to low heat for 4 hours or until the beans are tender. Add more water if necessary. Remove any foam from surface as it accumulates. Add chicken instant bouillon. Add salt and black pepper to taste. To serve, put 2 avocado slices in the bottom of each soup bowl. Add the hot soup. Sprinkle grated cheese on top and garnish with fresh chopped cilantro. Serves 6 to 8.

Note: Cuban-style Black Bean Soup is an alternate and equally delicious version. Make according to above directions. Add the chese but omit the cilantro. Instead, add a splash of vinegar and a sprinkling of fresh chopped green scallions to each serving.

TIFFANY'S BEAN POT SOUP

2   C. dried pinto beans
1   lb. cooked ham, diced
1   qt. water
1   22 oz. can tomato juice
4   C. chicken broth
3   onions, chopped
3   cloves garlic, minced
3   T. chopped parsley
¼   C. chopped green pepper
1   T. brown sugar
1   T. chili powder
1   t. MSG
1   t. salt
1   t. bay leaves, crushed
1   t. oregano
½   t. ground cumin seeds
½   t. rosemary leaves, crushed
½   t. celery seeds
½   t. ground thyme
½   t. marjoram
½   t. sweet basil
4   whole cloves
¾   to 1 C. dry sherry
green onions, chopped

Soak beans overnight. Wash and drain. Add all the other ingredients except the sherry and green onions. Bring to a boil and cook slowly until beans are tender. Add sherry. Serve in generous individual soup bowls and garnish with chopped green onions. Serves 8.

GARDEN FRESH VEGETABLE SOUP
(with an Italian touch)

¼ C. olive oil
2 onions, thinly sliced
2 cloves garlic, finely chopped
1 small eggplant, peeled and cubed (about 1½ C.)
2 medium-size zucchini, sliced
1 green pepper, seeded and diced
1 28 oz. can tomatoes (or fresh if it's the season)
1 qt. chicken broth, preferably homemade (see note)
1½ t. basil, crushed
½ t. coriander, crushed
salt and freshly ground black pepper to taste
4 oz. small shell macaroni, cooked and drained

Heat oil in a heavy kettle. Sauté the onions and garlic in it until transparent. Add the eggplant, zucchini and green pepper. Cook over medium heat, stirring often, until lightly browned (about 10 minutes). Add the remaining ingredients except macaroni. Bring to a boil, cover and simmer for 10 minutes or until vegetables are barely tender. Add macaroni and simmer 4 minutes longer. Serves 6.

Note: More chicken broth may be needed if mixture seems too thick.

Cream of Celery Soup

Cream of Cauliflower Soup

Cream of Carrot Soup

Cream of Parsley Soup

Cream of Artichoke Soup

Cream of Cucumber Soup

Cream of Lettuce Soup

Purée St. Germain

Spinach Bisque

Garden Fresh Cream of Tomato Soup

Tomato and Dill Soup

Wild Rice Autumn Soup

Mushroom Soup

Chicken Velvet Soup

Velvet Cheese Soup

Bongo Bongo

cream soups

CREAM OF CELERY SOUP

2   lbs. celery, finely chopped
4   T. butter
2   qts. chicken broth (preferably homemade)
1   lb. raw potatoes, peeled and sliced
salt and white pepper to taste
1   C. heavy cream
1   T. chopped parsley

Blanch celery. Drain. Melt butter. Add blanched celery and cook slowly for several minutes. Add chicken broth and potatoes. Bring to a boil and then simmer for 1 hour. Blend and strain (you may want to reserve some cooked, chopped celery to add to the finished soup). Return soup to kettle. Season. Before serving, add cream and chopped parsley. Serves 6 to 8.

Note: Freshly made croutons may be added.

CREAM OF CAULIFLOWER SOUP

1   large cauliflower
4   T. butter
2   qts. chicken broth or less, heated (see note)
1   lb. potatoes, peeled and sliced
salt and white pepper to taste
1   C. heavy cream
1   T. chopped parsley

Cut cauliflower into small pieces and blanch. Melt butter
in pot and add cauliflower. Cook slowly for a few minutes.
Add heated chicken broth and potatoes and bring to boil.
Simmer for 1 hour. Put through blender and strain, if neces-
sary. Return to stove. Add salt and white pepper to taste.
Stir in cream. Garnish with chopped parsley. Serves 8 to 10.

Note: If mixture seems too thin, add less chicken broth.

CREAM OF CARROT SOUP

4   T. butter
1   lb. carrots, washed, scraped and sliced
1   large onion, sliced
2   qts. chicken broth (see note)
1   C. uncooked rice
1   C. heavy cream
salt and white pepper to taste

Melt butter in large saucepan. Add carrots and onions and cook for 10 minutes over low flame, stirring often. Add the broth and rice and bring to a boil. Simmer for 1 hour. Purée in blender and strain if necessary. Stir in cream. Season to taste with salt and white pepper. Serves 8 to 10.

Note: If soup seems too thick, thin with additional chicken broth. However, this soup should be fairly thick.

CREAM OF PARSLEY SOUP

1½ lbs. zucchini
4   C. chicken broth
2   C. parsley, loosely packed (include a few tender stems)
1   C. heavy cream
salt and pepper to taste

Peel and cut up zucchini. Combine with chicken broth and cook until tender. Add parsley and cook 5 to 10 minutes longer. Put mixture through blender. Strain if necessary and return to pot. Slowly stir in heavy cream. Season with salt and pepper to taste. Serves 4 to 6.

Note: This also makes a very good watercress soup by substituting watercress for the parsley.

THOMAS EAKINS
  Portrait of Miss Gertrude Murray

CREAM OF ARTICHOKE SOUP

2   shallots, finely chopped
2   T. butter
2   T. flour
2   C. chicken broth
1 ¼ C. canned artichoke hearts, rinsed, drained and
      finely chopped
3   T. finely chopped parsley
1 ¼ C. light cream
salt and white pepper to taste

In a medium-size saucepan sauté the shallots until soft
in the butter. Slowly add the flour and cook, stirring constantly, for about 2 minutes. Remove from fire and stir
in the chicken broth, artichoke hearts and 2 tablespoons
of the chopped parsley. Return to fire and cook over
moderate heat, stirring, for 5 minutes. Purée the mixture,
in batches, in a blender. Strain through a coarse sieve
and return to cleaned saucepan. Set over moderate heat
and slowly add the cream, blending thoroughly. Season
with salt and white pepper to taste. The soup may be
served hot or cold. Garnish each serving with the remainder of the chopped parsley. Serves 4.

CREAM OF CUCUMBER SOUP

2   lbs. cucumbers (4 or 5 small)
½   C. shallots or onions, minced
3   T. butter
6   C. chicken broth (use canned if serving soup cold)
1½ to 2 T. white vinegar
¾   t. dried dill weed
4   T. Cream of Wheat
salt and white pepper
1   C. sour cream

Peel the cucumbers. Reserve half of a cucumber to be cut into slices for final decoration. Chop the rest into chunks. Sauté the shallots or onions in butter until soft. Add the cucumber chunks, broth, vinegar and dill weed. Bring to a boil and add the Cream of Wheat. Simmer for about 25 to 30 minutes. Purée in a blender and season with salt and white pepper. Beat in ½ cup of the sour cream. Pour into bowls and float slices of the reserved cucumber and a dollop of sour cream on each serving. Sprinkle on additional dill weed. May be served hot or cold. Serves 6 to 8.

CREAM OF LETTUCE SOUP

2   lbs. romaine lettuce
¾ C. green peas, fresh or frozen
6   T. butter
½ C. onion, chopped
4   T. flour
1   qt. heated chicken broth (see note)
salt and pepper
generous pinch of chervil
½ to ¾ C. heavy cream
sour cream (optional)

Wash, trim, chop and blanch the lettuce in salted water until it is wilted (set aside a little of the lettuce for garnish, if desired). Add peas to the blanching lettuce for a few minutes. Drain. Meanwhile, melt butter and sauté onions until soft. Add lettuce and pea mixture. Add flour and blend well. Stir in heated chicken broth. Cool for 10 to 15 minutes and taste for seasoning. Put mixture in blender and blend to desired texture. Add chervil and stir in the heavy cream. Serve hot or cold garnished with a dollop of sour cream or a bit of the reserved lettuce. Serves 6.

Note: Canned chicken broth should be used if serving cold.

PURÉE ST. GERMAIN

¾ C. butter
2 large leeks, white part only, chopped
1 large onion, chopped
2 heads of Boston lettuce, shredded
2 large uncooked potatoes, peeled and thinly sliced
5 C. chicken broth
4 C. fresh or frozen green peas
1 t. chervil
pinch of sugar
salt and pepper to taste
1½ C. light cream
½ C. heavy cream

Melt butter and add leeks, onion and lettuce. Simmer the vegetables for about 10 minutes. Add the potatoes and the broth and simmer about 20 minutes. Add the peas and chervil and simmer until peas are done (about 15 to 20 minutes for fresh peas and about 5 minutes for frozen peas). Purée the soup in a blender and return to pot. Season with sugar and salt and pepper to taste. Add the light cream. Whip the heavy cream, stirring in a little salt, and float a heaping tablespoon on each serving. Serves 6 to 8.

SPINACH BISQUE

3   T. butter
½ C. onion, chopped
3   T. flour
1   C. boiling water
1   10 oz. package frozen chopped spinach, thawed
2   T. instant chicken stock base
1   C. half and half cream
1   C. milk
dash of nutmeg
salt and white pepper to taste
finely grated Swiss cheese for garnish

Melt butter in heavy saucepan. Add and sauté onions until limp. Add flour slowly and stir until completely blended in and bubbly. Add boiling water gradually, stirring constantly until smooth. Purée spinach in blender and add to mixture along with chicken stock base. Simmer 5 minutes. Add the cream and milk and put through blender in batches. Return to cleaned saucepan and reheat. Add nutmeg and salt and white pepper to taste (it may not need salt) and stir well. Garnish each serving with a little of the cheese. Serves 4.

GARDEN FRESH CREAM OF TOMATO SOUP

2   onions, chopped
3   T. olive oil
4   large fresh tomatoes, peeled and cut in pieces
1   sprig fresh parsley
2   or 3 fresh basil leaves (or ¼ t. dried basil)
2   t. sugar
salt and pepper
1½ C. chicken broth (use canned chicken broth if
      soup is to be served cold)
1   C. sour cream

In a large saucepan sauté onions in olive oil until soft. Add tomatoes, parsley, basil, sugar, salt and pepper. Cover saucepan and simmer for 20 minutes, stirring occasionally. Force mixture through a fine sieve. Heat the chicken broth and slowly add the vegetable mixture to it. Remove from stove and allow to cool. Stir in sour cream. Adjust seasonings. Return to stove and barely bring to a boil. Serve as a hot soup or, when thoroughly chilled in the refrigerator, as a cold soup. Serves 4.

Note: This soup is definitely at its best when fresh tomatoes and fresh basil are in season.

TOMATO AND DILL SOUP

¼ C. vegetable oil
2 to 3 T. butter
3 medium onions, finely chopped
1 garlic clove, pierced by a wooden toothpick
7 to 8 large, firm tomatoes
¼ C. flour
2 T. (heaping) tomato paste
6 C. canned chicken broth, heated
2 C. heavy cream
salt and freshly ground white pepper
¼ to ½ C. chopped fresh dill (or 1 or 2 T. dried dill
    weed)

Heat oil and butter in large pan. Add the onion and garlic
and cook slowly without browning. Chop the tomatoes with
their skins on and add to the pan when the onions are
transparent. Cook the tomatoes quickly for 5 or 6 minutes,
stirring constantly. Remove the garlic clove. Add flour and
tomato paste and stir until smooth. Add the heated broth
little by little, stirring until thickened and smooth.
Simmer gently for 5 to 10 minutes. Put through a blender.
Strain, removing seeds and skins. Add the cream and the
salt and pepper to taste. Stir in the dill. May be served hot
or cold. Serves 8.

WILD RICE AUTUMN SOUP

1   medium onion, finely chopped
½ lb. fresh mushrooms, sliced
½ C. celery, thinly sliced
¼ C. butter
½ C. flour
6   C. chicken broth (preferably homemade)
2   C. cooked wild rice
½ t. curry powder
½ t. dried chervil
1   t. dry mustard
salt and white pepper to taste
2   C. half and half cream
¼ C. dry sherry
chopped chives or chopped parsley

Sauté the onions, mushrooms and celery in butter. Stir in the flour. Slowly add broth, stirring constantly. Continue stirring until mixture is slightly thickened. Add wild rice and seasonings. Reduce heat and stir in cream and sherry. Adjust seasonings and reheat but do not let boil. Garnish each serving with chopped chives or chopped parsley. Serves 6 to 8.

MUSHROOM SOUP

8   T. butter, softened
2   C. green onions, chopped (include about 4 inches
    of the green part on each onion)
2   T. flour
5   C. chicken broth
1   lb. fresh mushrooms (¾ lb. finely chopped for
    soup, the remainder cut into paper thin slices for
    garnish)
1½ C. heavy cream
salt and freshly ground black pepper

Combine softened butter and onions. Transfer to a kettle
and simmer, covered, for 15 to 20 minutes. Add flour and
make a roux. Add broth, a little at a time, stirring until it
thickens slightly. Add the chopped mushrooms and simmer,
partially covered, about 10 minutes. Purée the soup,
preferably in a food mill but a blender may be used. Return
the mixture to the kettle and stir in the cream, ½ cup at
a time until desired consistency is reached. Taste for
seasoning. To serve, place sliced mushrooms in tureen or
individual bowls and pour hot soup over them. Serves 6.

CHICKEN VELVET SOUP

1½ sticks butter
¾ C. flour
1   C. milk
1   C. heavy cream
6   C. chicken broth
2   C. finely chopped cooked chicken
salt and white pepper to taste
fresh parsley, chopped

Make a roux with the butter and flour and cook for 2 minutes. Heat milk, heavy cream and broth and add a little at a time to roux until mixture thickens. Blend until smooth. When soup starts to boil, add chicken and seasonings. Garnish with chopped parsley. Serves 6 to 8.

VELVET CHEESE SOUP

¾ C. onion, finely chopped
½ C. carrot, finely chopped
½ C. celery, finely chopped
⅓ C. green pepper, seeded and finely chopped
4 T. butter
4 T. flour
4 C. chicken broth, heated
4 C. (firmly packed) grated, aged Vermont Cheddar
    cheese
1 t. Dijon mustard
⅛ t. cayenne pepper
¼ to ⅓ C. heavy cream
salt

In a large saucepan sauté onion, carrot, celery and green pepper in butter for 10 minutes. Stir in the flour and cook for a few more minutes. Add the heated chicken broth, a little at a time. Bring to a slow boil, stirring often. Simmer, partially covered, for 30 minutes. Strain the mixture and return to saucepan. Stir in the grated cheese and continue to stir until completely melted. Add the mustard, cayenne pepper and heavy cream. Add salt to taste. Serves 6.

Real cheese lovers will find this smooth, creamy soup extraordinarily appealing.

BONGO BONGO

¼ C. onion, finely chopped
1 clove garlic, minced
4 T. butter
1 pint fresh oysters, chopped
4 T. flour
3 C. light cream
1 C. chicken broth
¾ C. spinach purée (puréed in blender from fresh or frozen spinach)
salt and pepper to taste

In a medium-size saucepan, sauté the onion and garlic in butter until soft. Add oysters and cook until they curl. With a slotted spoon, carefully remove oysters from mixture and set aside. Add flour to mixture and cook until foamy. Add cream and cook, stirring, until soup is thickened. Return oysters to mixture. Stir in chicken broth and spinach. Bring to boil. Remove from heat. Season to taste with salt and pepper. Serves 4 to 6.

Chilled Greek Vegetable Soup

Guadalajara Green Soup

Creamed Tomato Ice

Mint Pea Summer Soup

Margarita Gazpacho

Clear Gazpacho

Chilled Avocado Soup

Cold Tomato Soup

Senegalese Soup

Vichysoisse

Cool Green Summer Soup

Cold Shrimp and Tomato Soup with Dill

Cold Curried Cream of Eggplant Soup

chilled soups

CHILLED GREEK VEGETABLE SOUP

1   C. fresh mushrooms, quartered
2   medium-size ripe, fresh tomatoes, skinned and
    quartered
12 small, fresh pearl onions, halved or quartered
5   oz. dry white wine
3   oz. olive oil (more or less, according to taste)
10 oz. chicken broth (not homemade)
juice of 1 lemon
1   bay leaf
salt and pepper to taste
chopped parsley

Combine mushrooms, tomatoes, onions, wine, olive oil, chicken broth, lemon juice, bay leaf and salt and pepper in a medium-size saucepan. Bring just to a boil. Cover and simmer for 5 minutes. Remove from stove and allow to cool. Remove bay leaf and adjust seasonings. Cool in refrigerator for at least 3 hours. Serve very cold. Garnish each serving with chopped parsley. Serves 4.

GUADALAJARA GREEN SOUP

1   large ripe avocado, peeled, seeded and cut up
¼ of a medium-size onion, cut up
1   clove garlic, minced
juice of 1 lemon
⅛ t. Tabasco
½ t. Worcestershire Sauce
1   T. Picante Sauce
salt to taste
2½ C. chicken broth (not homemade)

Put all ingredients but chicken broth in blender. Blend briefly and then add chicken broth in a steady stream. Blend until smooth. Taste and add more salt, if necessary. Chill for at least 3 hours in refrigerator. Serves 4.

CREAMED TOMATO ICE

1   T. butter
1   onion, chopped
6   fresh tomatoes, peeled, seeded and chopped
½   C. canned chicken broth
½   t. tomato paste
½   t. thyme
½   t. sugar
¼   C. sour cream
¼   C. lime juice
salt and pepper
¾   C. heavy cream
6   lime slices
6   parsley sprigs

Melt butter in a saucepan and sweat onion. To sweat onion, cover with a buttered round of wax paper. Put lid on saucepan and cook over low heat for 15 minutes or until onion is soft. Remove wax paper and stir in tomatoes, chicken broth, tomato paste, thyme and sugar. Simmer mixture, covered, for 10 minutes. Let cool and put through blender or food processor and purée with sour cream, lime juice and salt and pepper to taste. Stir in heavy cream. Pour in individual soup bowls and chill in freezing compartment of refrigerator for 1 hour. Garnish each serving with a lime slice and sprig of parsley. Serves 6.

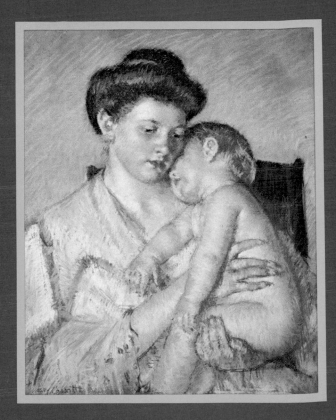

MARY CASSATT
Sleepy Baby

MINT PEA SUMMER SOUP

2   C. fresh peas (or two 10 oz. packages frozen
     peas), cooked
5   C. canned chicken broth
2   T. onion, chopped
4   T. soft butter
1 ½ C. loosely packed fresh mint leaves
dash of white pepper
salt to taste
Optional: 1 ½ C. heavy cream (see note)

Combine peas, chicken broth, onion, butter and mint leaves
(reserve six mint leaves for garnish). Place half of mixture
in blender. Cover and blend until well puréed. Repeat with
other half. Pour blended mixture into saucepan and bring
to a boil, stirring constantly. Strain and chill for at least 3
hours. Add salt and pepper after chilling. Serve in chilled
bowls and garnish each serving with a fresh mint leaf.
Serves 6.

Note: This soup may be made into a cream soup by stirring
      in the heavy cream before serving. It's delicious
      either way.

MARGARITA GAZPACHO

1   cucumber, peeled and chopped medium fine
1   small onion, chopped medium fine
2   ripe tomatoes, peeled and chopped medium fine
½   green pepper, seeded and chopped medium fine
1   clove garlic, chopped very fine or pressed
1   can tomato juice (46 oz.)
¼   C. cider vinegar
¼   C. olive oil
5   T. fresh lemon juice
3   T. green chili salsa (or 2 T. chopped green chili)
2   dashes Worcestershire Sauce
1   dash Tabasco
½   t. salt
¼   t. pepper
pinch of sugar
6   to 8 thin lemon slices

Mix all ingredients and chill for several hours or until icy cold. Garnish each serving with a thin lemon slice. Serves 6 to 8.

This delicious and popular soup is served at a unique family-run restaurant in Colorado Springs, Colorado.

CLEAR GAZPACHO

4   C. canned chicken broth, strained
2   C. dry white wine
½   C. lemon juice
3   small cucumbers, thinly sliced
3   fresh tomatoes, peeled, seeded and chopped
¾   C. scallions, thinly sliced
½   C. fresh parsley (or cilantro), minced
¼   t. Tabasco
salt and white pepper to taste

In a medium-size saucepan combine the chicken broth, wine and lemon juice. Bring the liquid to a boil and then let it cool to room temperature. Transfer the mixture to a large bowl and chill it, covered, in the refrigerator for at least 4 hours or overnight. Add the cucumbers, tomatoes, scallions and parsley (or cilantro). Add the Tabasco and the salt and white pepper to taste. Serve the soup in chilled bowls. Serves 6.

Note: This is a fresh and attractive-looking soup. It is particularly appetizing when served in clear glass or all-white bowls.

CHILLED AVOCADO SOUP

2   ripe avocados, seeded and peeled
1   C. or more canned chicken broth (see note)
6   T. sour cream
6   T. heavy cream
2   T. lime juice
½   t. salt
1 shallot, finely chopped
fresh cilantro, chopped (dried coriander may be substituted)

Put avocado meat, chicken broth, sour cream, heavy cream, lime juice, shallot and salt in blender. Whirl until puréed. Taste and add more salt if needed. Chill thoroughly. Serve in chilled bowls and garnish each serving with cilantro. Serves 4 to 6.

Note: The mixture will be very thick. If a thinner soup is desired, add more chicken broth. It is best not to make this soup more than 1 to 1½ hours in advance.

COLD TOMATO SOUP

3   C. tomato juice
2   T. tomato paste
4   small green onions, minced
pinch of powdered thyme
½ t. curry powder
2   T. lemon juice
grated rind of ½ lemon
dash of Tabasco Sauce
salt to taste
pinch of sugar
1   C. sour cream
chopped parsley

Carefully mix all ingredients together except sour cream
and parsley. Chill. Before serving, blend in the sour
cream and sprinkle each portion with chopped parsley.
Serves 4.

SENEGALESE SOUP

5   T. butter
1   onion, peeled and chopped
1   carrot, peeled and chopped
1   rib of celery, chopped
1   heaping t. curry powder
4   cans chicken broth
2   small cinnamon sticks
2   bay leaves
½   t. whole cloves
1   T. tomato purée
2   T. almond paste
1   T. currant jelly
3   T. flour
salt and white pepper to taste
2   C. heavy cream
1   package shredded coconut, toasted

Melt 2 T. butter in large saucepan. Add chopped onion, carrot and celery. Sauté gently until vegetables "color". Stir in curry powder. Slowly add chicken broth until mixture is smooth. Add cinnamon sticks, bay leaves, cloves, tomato purée, almond paste, currant jelly and salt and pepper. Bring slowly to a boil and simmer for one hour. Meanwhile mix the remaining 3 T. butter with the 3 T. flour until perfectly combined in a paste. After liquids have simmered for one hour, add flour-butter paste bit by bit, stirring constantly until smooth. Simmer until soup thickens. Strain and chill thoroughly in the refrigerator. To serve, blend in cream and garnish with toasted coconut. To toast coconut: spread evenly on a cookie sheet in a 250 degree oven — shake frequently and toast for about 45 minutes or until brown and crisp. Serves 6 to 8.

A smooth and subtle, cold curry soup.

VICHYSSOISE

6   leeks (white parts only), well washed and thinly sliced
3   onions, thinly sliced
½   stick butter
4   C. canned chicken broth
4   medium-size potatoes, peeled and thinly sliced
salt and white pepper to taste
2   C. milk
1   C. heavy cream
¼   t. nutmeg
chopped chives

Place the leeks and onions in a large saucepan with the butter. Put a buttered round of wax paper (or use the butter wrapper) over the vegetables. Put the lid on the saucepan and "sweat" the vegetables for 20 minutes or until they are well softened. Add chicken broth, potatoes and salt and white pepper to taste. Simmer the mixture until the potatoes are very soft. Purée the mixture through the medium disk of a food mill or in a blender. Add the milk, cream and nutmeg. Chill at least 3 hours. Serve the soup in chilled bowls. Garnish each serving with chopped chives. Serves 6.

COOL GREEN SUMMER SOUP

1   cucumber, peeled, seeded and cut into large
     pieces
½ of a ripe avocado, peeled, seeded and cut up
2   scallions, trimmed and sliced, using only the white
     and pale green parts
1   C. chicken broth (not homemade)
1   C. sour cream
3   T. fresh lime juice
dash of Tabasco
salt to taste

In a food processor fitted with the steel blade, combine
all ingredients. Spin for about 10 seconds or until mixture is just combined. Chill in refrigerator for at least
3 hours or until very cold. Serves 4.

Note: This is an easy, elegant and beautiful cool soup
      for any hot summer day.

COLD SHRIMP AND TOMATO SOUP WITH DILL

1   lb. small shrimp, cooked and shelled
1½ cucumbers, peeled, seeded and coarsely chopped
1   14 oz. can tomatoes with juice
1   T. dried dill weed
1   qt. buttermilk
1   C. tomato juice
salt to taste
Tabasco to taste
fresh or dried dill weed to garnish each serving

Combine shrimp, cucumber, canned tomatoes with juice and 1 T. dried dill weed in the container of a blender and mix well. In a large covered container, combine the above with the buttermilk, tomato juice, salt and Tabasco. Mix thoroughly. Chill completely. Garnish each serving with fresh or dried dill weed. Serves 8.

COLD CURRIED CREAM OF EGGPLANT SOUP

1 ¼ lbs. eggplant
½ C. chopped onion
¼ C. butter
1 T. curry powder
4 C. chicken broth
¾ C. heavy cream
salt and white pepper to taste
minced parsley

Trim and peel the eggplant and cut into ½ inch cubes. In a saucepan sauté the onion in the butter until it is soft. Stir in the curry powder and cook the mixture over moderately low heat, stirring, for 2 minutes. Add the eggplant and the chicken broth and bring the mixture to a boil over moderately high heat. Reduce heat and simmer, covered, for 45 minutes or until the eggplant is very soft. Transfer the mixture to a blender in batches and purée it. Strain into a bowl and add the cream and salt and white pepper. Let cool down and then chill in refrigerator, covered, for at least 3 hours. Serve in chilled bowls and garnish with chopped parsley. Serves 4.

Black Bean Soup

Quick Onion Soup

Avocado and Tomato Cream Consommé

Emergency Bisque

Lemon Mint Summer Soup

Cool Cucumber and Beet Borscht

Cream Cheese and Tomato Soup

Tomato and Clam Broth with Tarragon

Jellied Consommé in Avocado Halves

Clam Bisque

Curried Cream of Shrimp Soup

Gazpacho

quick soups

BLACK BEAN SOUP

2   cans Campbell's Black Bean Soup
1   can beef bouillon
2   soup cans water
½   small onion, minced (use 1 shallot, if available)
1   small carton sour cream
dry sherry to taste
salt and pepper if needed
4   to 6 thin lemon slices

Combine soup, bouillon, water and onion in saucepan. Stirring often, simmer until onion is soft. Let soup cool to lukewarm and stir in sour cream. Add sherry and also salt and pepper if needed. Reheat. Float a lemon slice on each serving. Serves 4 to 6.

This soup is quick and easy but the result is outstanding.

QUICK ONION SOUP

6   medium onions, thinly sliced
1   t. sugar
3   shakes ground nutmeg
1   stick butter or margarine
8   t. meat extract (B-V)
7   C. boiling water
½ C. dry sherry
salt
croutons (plain)
Gruyère or Swiss cheese, grated

Sauté onions, sugar and nutmeg in melted butter. Cook until onions are transparent but not browned. Dissolve meat extract in boiling water in a large saucepan. Add onion mixture and simmer for about 20 minutes. Add sherry during the last 2 minutes of cooking. Taste and add salt if needed. Spoon into individual, oven-proof soup bowls. Add croutons and top with grated cheese. Run under broiler for about 5 minutes or until cheese is melted and lightly browned. Serves 6 to 8.

AVOCADO AND TOMATO CREAM CONSOMMÉ

1   large avocado, peeled, seeded and cut up
2   t. lime juice
1   C. sour cream
2   cans beef consommé, chilled
1   fresh ripe tomato, peeled, seeded and chopped
salt to taste
dash of Tabasco
chopped parsley for garnish

In a food processor fitted with the steel blade, briefly blend avocado, lime juice and sour cream. Add the chilled consommé and briefly blend again. Add the chopped tomato and turn on processor just a few seconds (just long enough to integrate the 5 ingredients but to keep the tomato in small, visible pieces). Stir in salt and Tabasco to taste. Place in small individual bowls, cover and refrigerate for at least 3 hours. Garnish each serving with chopped parsley. Makes 6 to 8 small servings.

EMERGENCY BISQUE

1   can Campbell's Tomato Bisque, undiluted
1   can Campbell's Green Pea Soup, undiluted
1 ½ soup cans of milk
any amount of cooked crab meat, chicken meat or
    sliced sausage meat
2   T. sherry
salt and pepper to taste
chopped parsley for garnish

Combine first 2 ingredients in saucepan over medium
heat. Add milk, mixing thoroughly. Add crab meat,
chicken meat or sausage meat. Mix in sherry and add
salt and pepper, if needed. Heat thoroughly. Garnish
each serving with chopped parsley. Serves 4.

LEMON MINT SUMMER SOUP

1   can Campbell's Cream of Chicken soup
1   can chicken broth
grated rind of ½ lemon
juice of 2 lemons
5   fresh, whole mint leaves (or 1 t. dried mint)
salt to taste
dash of Tabasco
4   or 5 thin lemon slices
4   or 5 whole mint leaves (or 1 t. dried mint)

Combine all but last two ingredients in blender until mixture is smooth. Chill thoroughly in refrigerator. Float a thin lemon slice, topped by a fresh mint leaf or dried mint, on each portion before serving. Serves 4 to 5.

Note: Don't let the simplicity fool you. It's unbeatable on a
        hot summer day.

JELLIED CONSOMMÉ IN AVOCADO HALVES

2 cans Cross and Blackwell's red consommé Madrilène,
      chilled (see note)
2   avocados, peeled, seeded and halved
dollop of sour cream for each serving
1   small jar red or black caviar

Spoon chilled Madrilène into avocado halves. Put a dollop of sour cream on each. Top with red or black caviar. Serves 4.

Note: Beef consommé may be substituted but the red consommé Madrilène is particularly nice because of its color.

CLAM BISQUE

1   qt. canned clams
1   garlic clove, crushed
⅓   C. onion, finely chopped
½   C. butter
2½ C. half and half cream (use milk if you prefer it
     less rich)
2½ C. heavy cream
½   C. soft bread crumbs
salt and white pepper to taste
3 oz. dry sherry, warmed
chopped parsley

Drain clams, saving juice. Mix clams with the garlic and onions. Sauté in butter on low heat until clams curl. Add half and half, heavy cream and some of the reserved clam juice (which has been previously heated). Add bread crumbs and season to taste with salt and white pepper. Let stand over hot water for at least 15 minutes before serving. Just before serving, add the heated sherry. Garnish with chopped parsley. Serves 4 to 6.

CURRIED CREAM OF SHRIMP SOUP

2   cans cream of shrimp soup
1½ cans light cream
½   C. dry white wine
2   t. curry powder
salt and pepper, if needed

Combine shrimp soup, cream and wine in a saucepan.
Cook and stir over low fire until well heated and smooth.
Stir in curry powder and add salt and pepper, if needed.
Bring to a boil. Serves 4 to 6.

GAZPACHO

Mix in blender until smooth:
1   10 oz. can Snap-E-Tom
1   medium-size cucumber, peeled and coarsely
     chopped
1   medium-size tomato, peeled and coarsely chopped
1   T. sugar
¼   C. cider vinegar
¼   C. salad oil

Add to the above by hand (do not use blender):
2   10 oz. cans Snap-E-Tom
1   small onion, finely chopped
½   medium-size tomato, peeled and finely chopped
½   medium-size cucumber, peeled and finely chopped

Chill for at least 1 hour. Serves 6.

Bouillabaisse

Cioppino

Oyster Stew

Savory Clam Chowder

New England Fish Chowder

Shrimp Cheese Chowder

Creole Seafood Gumbo

seafood soups

BOUILLABAISSE

6 T. olive oil
1½ stalks celery, chopped
1 medium onion, chopped
2 cloves garlic, finely chopped
2 leeks, diced (white parts only)
1 t. thyme
1 large bay leaf
2 C. canned tomatoes, crushed
6 C. homemade fish stock (see Index for recipe)
1½ C. dry white wine
2 pinches saffron
salt and pepper to taste
4 T. fresh parsley, chopped

¾ lb. red snapper, cut into serving pieces (if un-available, use substitute)
1 lobster tail (leave in shell and cut in 1 inch pieces)
1 dozen little neck or small cherrystone clams in shells, well scrubbed
¾ lb. Alaskan King Crab meat (or substitute)
1 dozen jumbo shrimp, shelled, deveined and cut lengthwise down middle
olive oil and parmesan cheese (see note)

Heat the oil in a large kettle. Add the celery, onion, garlic, leeks, thyme and bay leaf and cook for 5 minutes. Add the tomatoes, fish stock, white wine, saffron, salt, pepper and parsley. Simmer for 15 minutes. To this point the recipe can be made ahead of time. Twenty minutes or so before serving, return the mixture to the boil and add the red snapper and cook about 5 minutes. Add the lobster and simmer about 8 minutes. Add clams, crab and shrimp. Cook, stirring gently, about 5 minutes or until the clam shells open. Serve in warmed soup bowls. Serves 6.

Note: For garnish, blend olive oil and parmesan cheese into a smooth paste. Pass at table and drop by spoonfuls into soup. Also serve croûtes with the soup (see Index for recipe).

CIOPPINO

½ C. olive oil
1 T. garlic, chopped
1 T. fresh parsley, chopped
1 T. celery, chopped
1 T. green pepper, seeded and chopped
2 C. canned tomatoes
1 C. tomato purée
salt and pepper to taste
paprika
1 C. dry red table wine
a few leaves of fresh sweet basil (or ¼ t. dried basil leaves)
2 dozen clams in shells
3 lbs. filleted fish (bass, cod, haddock or red snapper)
1 lb. raw shrimp, shelled and deveined
1 small lobster or crab in shell (or 2 lobster tails in shells)

Heat olive oil in large kettle. Sauté garlic, parsley, celery and green pepper until lightly browned. Add tomatoes and tomato purée. Season to taste with salt, pepper and paprika. Add wine and basil. Simmer for 1 hour. While mixture is simmering, wash and scrub clams. Steam in very little water just until the shells open. Strain the liquid in the pan from the clams and add to the sauce mixture. Cut filleted fish into small pieces. Cut up lobster with shell (or clean and break up crab). After sauce is cooked, add prepared fish, lobster or crab, and shrimp. Cook until all are done. Add clams at the very last. Serves 6.

Cioppino is a fish stew that seems to be native to the northern California coast. It is served to many a tourist on Fisherman's Wharf in San Francisco but originally it was a dish evolved by local fishermen from the day's catch.

OYSTER STEW

¼ C. onion, minced
1 garlic clove, minced
4 T. butter
1 T. fresh parsley, minced
1 lb. oysters, with liquid
1 pt. sour cream
1 C. half and half cream
Worcestershire Sauce
dash of red pepper
salt and pepper to taste
toasted oyster crackers

Sauté onion and garlic in butter until onion is transparent. Stir in parsley. Add oysters (if the oysters are large, cut in half) and simmer for 5 minutes. Allow mixture to cool down. Add sour cream, half and half cream, Worcestershire Sauce, red pepper and also salt and pepper to taste. Heat but DO NOT BOIL. Serve with toasted oyster crackers. Serves 4.

SAVORY CLAM CHOWDER

2   dozen small littleneck clams in shells
¼   C. salt pork or bacon, diced
½   C. onion, minced
1   C. water
1   large potato, peeled and diced
1   C. heavy cream
pinch of thyme
salt and white pepper to taste
toasted oyster crackers

Scrub the clams thoroughly and rinse. Put about an inch of water in a large kettle. Cover and steam the clams over medium to low heat until the shells open. Remove clams from the shells and reserve the broth left in the pan. Sauté salt pork or bacon until crisp. Remove to absorbent paper and reserve. Sauté onion in the fat. Add reserved clam broth to pan with onion and add water and diced potatoes. Cook until potatoes are tender. Add clams, cream, thyme and season to taste with salt and pepper. Do not allow to boil. Garnish with either the crisp salt pork or bacon. Serve with toasted oyster crackers. Serves 4.

NEW ENGLAND FISH CHOWDER

2 lbs. haddock (in areas where haddock is not
   available, cod, red snapper or trout may be
   substituted)
2 C. water
2 oz. salt pork, diced
2 onions, sliced
4 large potatoes, peeled and diced
1 C. celery, chopped
1 bay leaf, crumbled
salt and freshly ground black pepper
1 qt. milk
2 T. butter

Simmer haddock in water for 15 minutes (cooking time
should be reduced when using substitute fish because
haddock has firmer texture and takes a longer time to
cook). Drain fish, reserving broth. Remove bones from fish
and cut into bite-size pieces. Sauté diced salt pork until
crisp. Remove from pan and set aside. Sauté onions in pork
fat until golden brown. Add fish, potatoes, celery, bay leaf,
salt and freshly ground black pepper. Pour in reserved fish
broth plus enough boiling water to make 3 cups of liquid.
Simmer for 30 minutes. Stir in milk and butter and simmer
for 5 minutes. Adjust seasonings. Garnish chowder with
crisp diced salt pork. Serves 6.

SHRIMP CHEESE CHOWDER

2   C. onion, thinly sliced
2   T. butter or margarine
2   T. flour
1½ C. water, heated
2   C. potatoes, peeled and diced
1   C. celery, sliced
salt and pepper to taste
1   lb. cooked shrimp
2   C. milk
2½ C. (10 oz.) shredded sharp natural Cheddar cheese
2   T. sherry

Sauté onions in butter until tender. Slowly blend in flour. Stir in water, potatoes, celery and seasonings. Cover and simmer for 20 minutes or until potatoes are tender. Add remaining ingredients. Stir until cheese is completely melted. Taste for seasoning. Serves 6 to 8.

1½ to 2 C. roux (see recipe below)
1½ qts. boiling water
3½ C. fresh tomatoes, peeled and chopped (canned tomatoes may be substituted)
1 bay leaf
1 T. fresh parsley, chopped
¼ t. thyme
salt
Worcestershire Sauce
Tabasco
½ C. catsup, heated
1 lb. fresh okra, sliced
½ to 1 lb. fresh crabmeat (carefully picked over to remove bits of shell and cartilage)
1 lb. raw, medium-size shrimp, peeled and deveined
1½ t. filé
8 to 10 C. hot, steamed rice

Heat roux slowly in large kettle. Gradually stir in boiling water. Continue stirring until smooth. Add tomatoes, bay leaf, parsley and thyme. Season with salt, Worcestershire Sauce and Tabasco. Stir in heated catsup. Cook slowly on top of stove for 3 hours. Add sliced okra and cook for about 15 minutes or until okra is tender. Stir often. Add crabmeat and shrimp and cook for 30 minutes. Remove bay leaf. Adjust seasonings. Remove from stove and stir in filé (see note). Serve over hot, steamed rice in warmed soup bowls. Serves 8 to 10.

Note: Gumbo must never be boiled after the filé has been added or it will become ropey. To reheat, it may be slowly simmered or kept hot over warm water. Also, never add black pepper to seafood gumbo.

Roux

½ C. bacon drippings
1 C. flour
1 clove garlic, chopped fine
2 or 3 stalks celery, chopped fine
1 large onion, chopped fine

Roux is best made in an iron skillet or pot. Brown flour in bacon drippings very slowly until it is dark brown. You can detect when it is done by the different odor. Do not let burn or allow to stick. Stir constantly. This will take a long time. Add celery, onion and garlic and simmer for 30 minutes. Yields 1½ to 2 cups. Roux may be made ahead of time and frozen to thaw and use later.

Chilled Raspberry Soup

Cold Peach Soup with
Fresh Blueberry Garnish

Cool Strawberry Wine Soup

Orange Almond Bisque

Walnut Soup

Cream of Pecan Soup

Purée of Pumpkin Soup

Butternut Squash and Apple Soup

Scandinavian Fruit Soup

Cool Plum Wine Soup

Orange, Tomato and Ginger Consommé

exotic soups

CHILLED RASPBERRY SOUP

3½ C. fresh raspberries (or 3 ten oz. packages of
    frozen raspberries)
3½ C. water
1   C. Rosé wine
dash of salt
¾ C. sugar (or less depending on sweetness of wine)
1   C. sour cream
6   lime slices

Mash raspberries and force through a fine sieve or blend
in the blender. Strain the mixture to remove seeds. (If using
frozen berries, thaw and strain berries, saving juice. Add
enough water to juice to make 3½ C. liquid. Use instead
of the 3½ C. water.) Add water, wine, salt and sugar. Bring
to a boil and simmer, tightly covered, for 5 minutes. Cool.
Add sour cream and stir until thoroughly blended. Chill.
Serve in chilled cups. Garnish each serving with a lime
slice. Serves 6.

GEORGE BELLOWS
 Emma in a Purple Dress

COLD PEACH SOUP WITH
FRESH BLUEBERRY GARNISH

1½ C. water
4   cloves
¾ C. sugar
1   cinnamon stick, broken into pieces
2   T. cornstarch mixed with ¼ C. cold water
1½ C. dry white wine
3   lbs. ripe peaches
1   C. fresh blueberries
1   C. heavy cream

Pour water into a small saucepan. Add the cloves, sugar
and cinnamon. Bring to a boil. Reduce heat and simmer
for 10 minutes. Add the diluted cornstarch, whipping it into
the syrup with a wire whisk. Bring the syrup to a boil again.
Remove from stove, stir in the wine and refrigerate. Wash
and peel the peaches. Split lengthwise and remove the
seeds. Slice enough of the best peaches to make about
2 cups. Remove the cloves and cinnamon from the syrup.
Add the sliced peaches to the syrup. Chop the remainder
and purée in the blender. Add to the syrup mixture. Chill
thoroughly. To serve, ladle into chilled bowls, sprinkle with
blueberries and garnish with a generous dollop of whipped cream. Serves 6 to 8.

COOL STRAWBERRY WINE SOUP

1   qt. strawberries, washed thoroughly and hulled
3   T. dry white wine
2   C. plain yogurt
¼   C. (or more) confectioners sugar

Whirl berries in blender with wine. Strain through sieve to remove seeds. Put mixture back in blender with yogurt and sugar. The amount of sugar used will depend on the sweetness of the berries. Chill for 45 minutes to 1 hour. This soup is best when not allowed to set too long. Serves 4 to 6.

This soup is delicious served as a first course for a summer dinner party or with a light summer lunch salad plate.

ORANGE ALMOND BISQUE

2   C. almonds, blanched
3   C. canned chicken broth
1   T. onion, grated
1   bay leaf
4   T. grated orange rind
4   egg yolks
1   C. heavy cream
salt and white pepper
¼   C. dry sherry

Pulverize almonds in blender or food grinder. In large saucepan, combine almonds with chicken broth, onion, bay leaf and 2 T. of the grated orange rind. Simmer, uncovered, for 30 minutes. Meanwhile, combine egg yolks, heavy cream, salt and white pepper in bowl and beat together. Remove almond mixture from stove and allow to cool slightly. Discard bay leaf. Put through blender until smooth. Combine almond and egg mixture. Return to stove and reheat over a low flame, taking care not to boil or egg yolks will curdle. Stir in sherry and adjust seasonings. Chill thoroughly. Garnish each serving with remainder of grated orange rind. Serves 4 to 6.

WALNUT SOUP

6   C. beef stock or canned bouillon
2   T. butter
2   T. flour
1½ C. finely ground walnuts
½   t. salt (or to taste)
freshly ground pepper
½   t. Worcestershire Sauce
2   dashes Tabasco
2   T. dry white wine or dry Madiera

Pour beef stock in a saucepan and bring to a boil. Remove from heat. In large saucepan, melt butter and stir in flour with a whisk until a smooth paste is formed. Continue to stir and pour in the hot beef stock a little at a time. Add ground walnuts, salt, pepper, Worcestershire and Tabasco and simmer for 30 minutes. Add the wine or Madiera during the last 10 minutes. Serves 6.

CREAM OF PECAN SOUP

1½ C. pecans
6   C. beef consommé
1   beef bouillon cube
1   T. onion, chopped finely
1   clove garlic, minced
½ C. butter
½ C. tomato paste
1   T. cornstarch
salt and pepper to taste
dash of nutmeg
1   egg yolk
½ C. heavy cream

Combine pecans, consommé and bouillon cube in blender. Sauté onion and garlic in butter until limp. Slowly add nut mixture, tomato paste and cornstarch that has been moistened with a little water. Cook slowly for 30 minutes, stirring often. Let mixture cool down. Add salt, pepper and nutmeg. Beat egg yolk with cream and add to the soup. Reheat. Serves 4 to 6.

PURÉE OF PUMPKIN SOUP

1   onion, chopped
2   T. chopped leeks, white part only
2   T. butter
2   C. chicken broth
2   C. unsweetened canned pumpkin (or puréed,
    cooked fresh pumpkin)
½   t. sugar
½   t. mace
¼   t. nutmeg
salt and white pepper to taste
half and half cream to taste
½   C. heavy cream, whipped and salted

Sauté onion and leek in butter until transparent. Stir in broth
and pumpkin and heat thoroughly. Purée the mixture in a
blender. Strain, if necessary. Add sugar, mace and nutmeg.
Add salt and white pepper to taste. Blend again. Return
mixture to stove and slowly stir in half and half cream to
desired consistency. Garnish with salted whipped cream.
Serves 6.

BUTTERNUT SQUASH AND APPLE SOUP

1   small butternut squash (about 1 lb.)
3   tart green apples
1   medium onion
¼   t. dried rosemary or 1 sprig fresh rosemary
¼   t. dried marjoram or 1 sprig fresh marjoram
3   cans chicken broth
2   cans water
2   slices white bread
1   t. salt
¼   t. pepper
¼   C. heavy cream
chopped fresh parsley

Cut the butternut squash in half and scoop out seeds. Peel, core and chop the apples. Chop the onions. In a large saucepan combine all ingredients except cream and parsley. Bring to a boil. Simmer, uncovered, for 45 minutes. Remove butternut squash and scoop out the pulp from the peel, discarding peel. Add pulp back to mixture and purée in blender until smooth. Do this in several batches. Return mixture to saucepan and bring to a boil. Just before serving, mix in the cream. Serve hot and garnish each serving with chopped fresh parsley. Serves 8.

Note: This soup is also good served cold, but add more cream if doing so.

SCANDINAVIAN FRUIT SOUP

1   lb. prunes, pitted
¼   C. currants
1   C. white seedless raisins
2   qts. water
juice of lemon
½   C. pearl tapioca (for thinner soup use ¼ C.)
1   cinnamon stick
1   1 lb. can peach halves
1   1 lb. can apricot halves
1   1 lb. can pitted cherries
1   orange
1   lemon
1   T. cognac for each serving

Soak prunes, currants and raisins overnight in 2 qts. water and juice of 1 lemon. Place the soaked fruit and its liquid in a heavy kettle and combine with the tapioca (the tapioca should be soaked beforehand according to package directions). Add the cinnamon stick and cook for 1 hour. Add peach halves, apricot halves, cherries and their can juices. Cut orange and lemon into thin slices and cut those slices in half. Add these to kettle. Do not cook but heat all very slowly on simmer, stirring often to keep fruit from scorching. This must be done very carefully so as not to break up fruit. Remove cinnamon stick. Add cognac to each serving. Serves 12.

Note: This soup is traditionally served as a dessert in Scandinavian countries. In Germany the soup is thinner and is served in summertime as a chilled prelude to the entrée.

COOL PLUM WINE SOUP

1 lb. 13 oz. can of purple plums
1 C. water
⅔ C. sugar
1 cinnamon stick
¼ t. white pepper
pinch of salt
½ C. heavy cream
½ C. dry red wine
1 T. cornstarch
2 T. lemon juice
1 t. grated lemon rind
2 C. sour cream
3 T. brandy
cinnamon

Drain plums, reserving the syrup. Remove the pits and chop the plums. Combine plums, reserved syrup, water, sugar, cinnamon stick, white pepper and salt in a saucepan. Bring to boil over moderately high heat. Reduce heat and cook for 5 minutes, stirring occasionally. Stir in heavy cream and wine which has been mixed with the cornstarch. Cook mixture until it is thickened, stirring constantly. Stir in lemon juice and lemon rind and remove pan from heat. Let mixture cool down. In a small bowl whisk one cup of the sour cream into the brandy and stir both into the soup, mixing until well blended. Let soup come to room temperature. Chill, covered, in the refrigerator for at least 4 hours. Ladle soup into chilled cups. Garnish each serving with a dollop of sour cream and a sprinkling of cinnamon. Serves 6 to 8.

Note: This beautiful and unusual soup is of Hungarian origin.

ORANGE, TOMATO AND GINGER CONSOMMÉ

4½ C. chicken broth, strained
½ C. orange juice (preferably fresh)
rind of 1 orange, cut into julienne strips
enough drained ginger (in syrup), cut into julienne
strips, to measure 2 T.
1 T. tomato paste
4 tomatoes, peeled, seeded and cut into julienne
strips
¼ t. powdered ginger
salt and pepper to taste
fresh mint leaves, chopped
4 to 6 orange slices, seeds removed

In a large saucepan combine the chicken broth, orange juice, orange rind, drained ginger strips and tomato paste. Bring to a boil and simmer for 5 minutes. Stir the tomatoes, powdered ginger and salt and pepper into the soup mixture. Place over medium heat for 5 minutes or until thoroughly heated. Garnish each serving with an orange slice sprinkled with chopped mint leaves. Serves 4 to 6.

Note: The unusual combination of ingredients makes this a first course soup that is not only elegant in appearance but tantalizingly aromatic.

Sopa de Arroz con Gallina

Sopa de Tortilla

Waterzooi

Green Waterzooi

Avgolemono

Soupe à l'Oignon

Chavela

Pozole

Hot and Sour Soup

Snow Pea Soup

Gazpacho

Pasta e Fagioli

Minestrone

Zuppa di Pasta

foreign soups

SOPA DE ARROZ CON GALLINA
(Mexican)

4   T. oil
1   C. uncooked rice
1   medium onion, minced
½ C. tomato sauce
2   qts. heated chicken broth, preferably homemade
salt and white pepper to taste
1   to 2 C. cooked chicken cut in bite-sized pieces

Heat oil and brown rice lightly in it. Add onion, tomato
sauce, broth and salt and pepper. Cover tightly and simmer
for 30 minutes. During the last 10 minutes of cooking, add
the chicken pieces. Serves 6 to 8.

Tortillas filled with guacamole make a delicious accompani-
ment for this soup.

SOPA DE TORTILLA (Mexican)

4	tortillas
4	T. cooking oil
1	small onion, finely chopped
4	oz. can tomato sauce
4	C. chicken broth (preferably homemade)

salt to taste
Tabasco to taste
Chopped fresh cilantro (dried coriander may be substituted)
6   lime slices

Cut tortillas in quarters, then strips and fry in oil. Drain on paper towels. In the same pan sauté onions until transparent. Stir in tomato sauce and chicken broth. Bring to a boil, reduce heat and simmer for 30 minutes. Add half of the tortilla strips and just heat through. Put the remaining tortilla strips in individual soup bowls and pour the soup over. Sprinkle with cilantro. Serve with a slice of lime. Serves 6.

WATERZOOI (Belgian)

4 T. butter
4 large leeks, white parts only, chopped
4 celery stalks, chopped
2 carrots, chopped
1 onion, chopped
3 parsley sprigs
⅛ t. ground nutmeg
⅛ t. ground thyme

1 bay leaf
1 4 lb. roasting chicken
6 to 8 C. chicken broth or veal stock, preferably homemade
3 egg yolks
½ C. heavy cream
juice of 1 lemon
salt and freshly ground pepper

Melt butter in a large heavy casserole or kettle. Add the leeks, celery, carrot, onion, parsley sprigs, nutmeg, thyme and bay leaf. Stirring constantly, cook about 5 minutes or until the vegetables are semi-soft. Do not let brown. Lay the chicken on top of the vegetables and add enough broth or stock to cover. Cover with lid and bring to a boil. Simmer for about 45 minutes to 1 hour or until chicken is tender. Remove chicken from broth and skin. Discard skin. Bone chicken and cut meat into as large pieces as possible. Keep warm in a 250° oven. Strain broth into a saucepan. Place over high heat and reduce to 4 cups. In a heated soup tureen, beat together the egg yolks and the heavy cream. Slowly stir in the reduced broth and the lemon juice. Season to taste with salt and pepper. Add the chicken pieces and serve immediately. Serves 4.

Note: Waterzooi is a famous, traditional dish from Belgium. There are a number of different variations. The Green Waterzooi on the next page is one. Waterzooi can also be made with fish or rabbit. Although requiring an extra bit of time and effort, both of these soups are exceptional.

GREEN WATERZOOI (Belgian)

4 T. butter
4 large leeks, white parts only, chopped
4 celery stalks, chopped
2 carrots, chopped
1 onion, chopped
3 parsley sprigs
⅛ t. ground nutmeg
⅛ t. ground thyme
1 bay leaf
1 4 lb. roasting chicken
6 to 8 C. chicken broth or veal stock, preferably homemade
3 egg yolks
½ C. heavy cream
juice of 1 lemon
salt and freshly ground pepper
¼ C. minced fresh chervil (or 1 T. dried chervil)
¼ C. minced fresh parsley

Melt butter in a large heavy casserole or kettle. Add the leeks, celery, carrot, onion, parsley sprigs, nutmeg, thyme and bay leaf. Stirring constantly, cook about 5 minutes or until the vegetables are semi-soft. Do not let brown. Lay the chicken on top of the vegetables and add enough broth or stock to cover. Cover with lid and bring to a boil. Simmer for about 45 minutes to 1 hour or until chicken is tender. Remove chicken from broth and skin. Discard skin. Bone chicken and cut meat into as large pieces as possible. Keep warm in a 250⁰ oven. Strain broth. Purée vegetables from strained broth in a blender or push through a fine sieve. Reduce broth to 4 cups by placing over high heat. Add these 4 cups of broth to the puréed vegetables and blend well. Beat together the egg yolks and heavy cream and gradually stir into the mixture. Stir in lemon juice, chervil and parsley. Add the chicken pieces and serve immediately. Serves 4.

AVGOLEMONO (Greek)

6 C. chicken broth
¼ C. uncooked rice
1 t. salt
3 eggs
¼ C. lemon juice
1 lemon, thinly sliced

Combine broth, rice and salt. Bring to boil and reduce heat. Cover and simmer until rice is just tender. Remove from heat. In a bowl beat eggs until fluffy and pale yellow. Beat in lemon juice. Slowly stir about 2 cups of the hot broth into the lemon-egg mixture and whisk vigorously. Pour this mixture back into rest of soup. Whisk it until slightly thickened (about the consistency of heavy cream). Cool to room temperature. Refrigerate until icy cold. Stir before serving. Garnish each serving with a lemon slice. Serves 4 to 6.

GEORGES ROUAULT
Woman's Head

GREEN WATERZOOI (Belgian)

4   T. butter
4   large leeks, white parts only, chopped
4   celery stalks, chopped
2   carrots, chopped
1   onion, chopped
3   parsley sprigs
⅛   t. ground nutmeg
⅛   t. ground thyme
1   bay leaf
1   4 lb. roasting chicken
6   to 8 C. chicken broth or veal stock, preferably
    homemade
3   egg yolks
½   C. heavy cream
juice of 1 lemon
salt and freshly ground pepper
¼   C. minced fresh chervil (or 1 T. dried chervil)
¼   C. minced fresh parsley

Melt butter in a large heavy casserole or kettle. Add the
leeks, celery, carrot, onion, parsley sprigs, nutmeg, thyme
and bay leaf. Stirring constantly, cook about 5 minutes or
until the vegetables are semi-soft. Do not let brown. Lay
the chicken on top of the vegetables and add enough broth
or stock to cover. Cover with lid and bring to a boil. Simmer
for about 45 minutes to 1 hour or until chicken is tender.
Remove chicken from broth and skin. Discard skin. Bone
chicken and cut meat into as large pieces as possible. Keep
warm in a 250° oven. Strain broth. Purée vegetables from
strained broth in a blender or push through a fine sieve.
Reduce broth to 4 cups by placing over high heat. Add
these 4 cups of broth to the puréed vegetables and blend
well. Beat together the egg yolks and heavy cream and
gradually stir into the mixture. Stir in lemon juice, chervil
and parsley. Add the chicken pieces and serve
immediately. Serves 4.

AVGOLEMONO (Greek)

6   C. chicken broth
¼   C. uncooked rice
1   t. salt
3   eggs
¼   C. lemon juice
1   lemon, thinly sliced

Combine broth, rice and salt. Bring to boil and reduce heat. Cover and simmer until rice is just tender. Remove from heat. In a bowl beat eggs until fluffy and pale yellow. Beat in lemon juice. Slowly stir about 2 cups of the hot broth into the lemon-egg mixture and whisk vigorously. Pour this mixture back into rest of soup. Whisk it until slightly thickened (about the consistency of heavy cream). Cool to room temperature. Refrigerate until icy cold. Stir before serving. Garnish each serving with a lemon slice. Serves 4 to 6.

SOUPE À L'OIGNON (French)

1½ lbs. yellow onions, thinly sliced
3 T. butter
1 T. oil
1 t. salt
¼ t. sugar
3 T. flour
2 qts. beef bouillon, boiling
½ C. dry white wine
salt and pepper
3 T. cognac
6 to 8 rounds of hard-toasted French bread
6 to 8 slices of Swiss cheese

In a covered saucepan, cook the onions slowly in the butter and oil for 15 minutes. Remove the cover, raise heat to moderate, and add 1 teaspoon salt and the sugar. Cook for 30 to 40 minutes, stirring frequently, until the onions have turned an even, deep, golden brown. Add flour and stir for 2 minutes. Remove from heat and blend in boiling beef bouillon. Add the white wine and season to taste with salt and pepper. Simmer, partially covered, for 30 to 40 minutes or more. Just before serving, stir in cognac. Place a round of hard-toasted French bread in the bottom of each individual, oven-proof soup bowl. Pour in soup. Cover with a slice of Swiss cheese. Run bowls under broiler until cheese starts to melt. Serves 6 to 8.

Note: This soup takes about 2½ hours from start to finish. When making onion soup, it is necessary for the onions to be cooked a long, slow time in butter and oil and simmered in broth for an equally long time. This allows the onions to develop the deep rich flavor characteristic of traditional French onion soup.

CHAVELA (Mexican)

1 T. olive oil
¾ to 1 C. chopped onion
½ t. garlic
2 C. Italian peeled tomatoes
1 C. carrots, peeled and cubed
1 C. celery, scraped and cubed
8 C. fish stock
2 bay leaves
salt and pepper to taste

1 C. raw potatoes, peeled and cubed
1 skinless, boneless fish fillet such as sea bass or snapper, cut into bite size pieces
1 lb. raw shrimp, peeled and deveined
1 pt. raw oysters
Salsa Picante (see below)
2 avocados, peeled, seeded and cubed
6 lime wedges

Heat oil in a kettle and cook onion until wilted. Add garlic and stir a few minutes. Add tomatoes, carrots, celery and stock. Add bay leaves and salt and pepper to taste. Bring to boil and simmer 20 minutes. Add potatoes and cook until tender, about 20 minutes. Add fish and simmer about 3 minutes. When ready to serve, bring the soup to a boil and add shrimp and oysters. Do not cook further. Remove from stove and let stand for 3 to 4 minutes. Ladle into soup bowls and top each with a spoonful of Salsa Picante and cubes of avocado. Serve with a wedge of lime. Serves 6.

SALSA PICANTE:

3 or 4 medium tomatoes
¾ C. chopped onion
¼ C. fresh cilantro

1 to 3 T. fresh green chilies, chopped
salt to taste

Do not peel the tomatoes. Cut in half and squeeze each half to remove seeds. Chop. Add the remaining ingredients and mix well.

Note: Although the fresh, homemade Salsa Picante is recommended, a good commercial brand may be substituted.

POZOLE (Mexican)

1   2 lb. pork roast, boned and cubed with fat removed
1   2 lb. chicken, disjointed
3   qts. water
2   large onions, chopped
2   cloves garlic, crushed
2   (or more) T. chili powder
1   bunch fresh parsley, chopped
1   or 2 canned chili chipoltes (depending on how hot
    you want mixture)
1   1 lb. can tomatoes
1½ T. sugar
salt and pepper
2   1 lb. cans hominy

Garnishes: avocado slices
           radish slices
           chopped green onions
           grated Monterrey Jack cheese
           tortilla chips

Put first 11 ingredients in large kettle and bring to a boil. Turn heat to low and simmer gently, covered, for 1 hour or until pork and chicken are tender. Add hominy and cook 15 minutes longer. Taste and correct seasonings if necessary. Serve with garnishes listed above. Serves 10 to 12.

Suggestion: This is delicious served with flour tortillas fried crisply in peanut oil.

HOT AND SOUR SOUP (Chinese)

2   qts. chicken broth
½ C. dried Chinese mushrooms, soaked in water for 30 minutes and with any tough stems cut away, sliced into thin strips
½ C. canned bamboo shoots, drained, rinsed and cut into thin strips
1   T. soy sauce (Kikkoman or Tamari)
½ lb. boneless pork, trimmed of all fat and cut into thin strips (This is easier to do if meat is slightly frozen)
2   squares Chinese bean curd (approximately ½" by 3" thick), drained and rinsed and cut into thin strips
½ t. white pepper
2   T. white vinegar
2   T. cornstarch mixed with 3 T. cold water
1   egg, slightly beaten
2   t. sesame seed oil
1   green onion (including top), finely chopped on the diagonal

Measure out all ingredients and have within easy reach. Make sure that you cut mushrooms, bamboo shoots, pork and bean curd in uniform matchstick size pieces. Combine broth, mushrooms, bamboo shoots, soy sauce and pork in a saucepan and bring to a boil. Reduce heat to simmer and cook 3 minutes. Add bean curd, pepper and vinegar. Bring to a boil again and reduce heat. Add cornstarch mixture and stir while soup thickens. Slowly add egg, stirring gently about 1 minute. Remove from heat and stir in sesame seed oil. Sprinkle chopped green onions on top. Serves 6 to 8.

Note: This soup may be made more "hot and sour" by adding more pepper and vinegar.

SNOW PEA SOUP (Chinese)

fresh ginger root (a piece approximately 1 inch square)
1   t. coriander
4   C. chicken broth, preferably homemade
10 to 12 snow peas (you can use frozen but fresh
      are better)
salt and white pepper

Add ginger root and coriander to chicken broth and simmer for 15 minutes. Remove ginger root. Cut snow peas in half crosswise. Slice halves into julienne strips. Add to broth mixture and heat through until cooked but still crisp. This does not take long. If using canned chicken broth, you may need to add salt and white pepper to taste. Serves 6.

GAZPACHO (Spanish)

3   ripe tomatoes, peeled and cut up
½   green pepper, seeded and cut up
½   small onion, chopped
1   clove garlic
3   T. vinegar
2   T. salad oil
1   t. salt
¼   t. pepper
½   C. water
1   cucumber, peeled and cut up
2   C. tomato juice

Mix tomatoes, green pepper, onion, garlic, vinegar, oil, salt, pepper and water in blender until smooth. Add cucumber and blend only until cucumber is crushed. Add tomato juice by hand. Do not blend any more. Chill thoroughly. Serves 5 or 6.

This recipe is best only when you can obtain good, red, ripe tomatoes in season.

PASTA E FAGIOLI (Italian)

1   lb. dried Great Northern (white) beans
salt to taste
1   C. olive oil (or ½ C. olive oil and ½ C. safflower
    oil)
1   clove garlic, unpeeled
1   bay leaf
½ lb. macaroni, uncooked
1   t. basil
1   t. coarsely ground hot red pepper
4   C. chicken broth
parsley, chopped
grated Parmesan cheese

Soak beans overnight in water to cover. Cook beans in same water. Bring to a slow boil, add salt. Skim off foam. Add oil, garlic and bay leaf. Turn heat down and cook until tender. Remove garlic and bay leaf. Cook the macaroni. Add it to the beans along with basil, red pepper and chicken broth. Simmer. Garnish with chopped parsley and grated cheese before serving. Serves 8.

MINESTRONE (Italian)

1 onion, sliced
2 slices bacon, diced
1 T. olive oil
1 carrot, scraped and diced
2 stalks celery, diced
1 large potato, peeled and cubed
1 C. white beans, soaked overnight
salt and pepper to taste
2 C. broth (1 cup chicken broth, 1 cup beef broth)
   (more broth may be needed during the cooking
   process)
1 T. tomato paste
1½ oz. Italian or Chinese dried mushrooms, soaked
   according to directions
1½ C. of any two of the following fresh vegetables:
   eggplant, quartered lengthwise and sliced
   green beans, snapped
   okra, sliced
   peas
   zucchini, sliced
1 small cabbage, shredded
3 T. Pesto (optional)
1 C. pasta (vermicelli or spaghetti) broken into small
   pieces
1¼ C. fresh spinach, chopped
1 C. freshly grated Parmesan

In a large saucepan, sauté onion and bacon in olive oil until tender. Add carrots, celery, potato, white beans, salt and pepper and broth. Simmer, uncovered, for 45 minutes. Add tomato paste, mushrooms and fresh vegetables. Bring to boil, lower heat, cover and simmer for 20 minutes. Add cabbage and cook until wilted (about 15 minutes). Add more broth if needed. Vegetables should be covered with broth but soup should remain thick. Stir in Pesto. Add pasta and spinach and simmer for 5 minutes. Stir in 1 or more spoonsful of grated Parmesan until mixture is thick and rich. Serve in heated soup tureen accompanied by the rest of the grated cheese. Serves 8.

ZUPPA DI PASTA (Italian)

9   C. chicken broth
1   stalk celery, diced
2   leeks, sliced thinly (use only white and light green
    parts)
2   large ripe tomatoes, peeled and cut up
1   C. Orzo (rice-shaped pasta)
1½ t. chopped fresh basil (or ½ t. dried basil)
2   eggs
2   T. cold water
½   C. grated parmesan or romano cheese
salt and white pepper to taste
chopped parsley

Combine broth with celery and leeks in a large saucepan.
Cover and simmer for about 15 minutes. Add tomatoes,
Orzo and basil and simmer for another 15 minutes.
Remove from fire and let cool down. Meanwhile beat
eggs, cold water and cheese together. Add slowly, stir-
ring constantly, to the cooled-down mixture in saucepan.
Season to taste with salt and white pepper. Reheat but
DO NOT BOIL. Garnish with chopped parsley. Serves 8.

INDEX

COOKBOOK ORDER FORM

REVISED EDITION

Gallery Buffet Soup Cookbook
Dallas Museum of Art
1717 North Harwood
Dallas, Texas 75201

Please send _____ copies . . $12.50 each _____
Postage and Handling . . . . 1.75 each _____
Texas residents add 5% tax . . . .63 each _____
Enclosed is my check or
money order . . . . TOTAL _____
Make checks payable to: Gallery Buffet Soup Cookbook
Name _____
Street _____
City and State _____ Zip _____

COOKBOOK ORDER FORM

REVISED EDITION

Gallery Buffet Soup Cookbook
Dallas Museum of Art
1717 North Harwood
Dallas, Texas 75201

Please send _____ copies . . $12.50 each _____
Postage and Handling . . . . 1.75 each _____
Texas residents add 5% tax . . . .63 each _____
Enclosed is my check or
money order . . . . TOTAL _____
Make checks payable to: Gallery Buffet Soup Cookbook
Name _____
Street _____
City and State _____ Zip _____